LearningWebs
Curriculum Journeys on the Internet

Michele Keating

Jon W. Wiles

Mary Wood Piazza

with illustrations by
Steve Robertson

Merrill
Prentice Hall

Upper Saddle River, New Jersey
Columbus, OH

Library of Congress Cataloging in Publication Data

Keating, Michele.
    LearningWebs: curriculum journeys on the Internet / by Michele Keating, Jon W. Wiles,
Mary Wood Piazza.
        p. cm.
    ISBN 0-13-031919-8
        1. Internet—Study and teaching. 2. Education—Computer network sources. 3.
Teaching—Computer network resources. 4. Internet in education. I. Wiles, Jon. II.
Piazza, Mary. III. Title.

TK5105.875.I57 K435 2002
371.33'4478—dc21

                                                                                    2001032866

Vice President and Publisher: Jeffery W. Johnston
Executive Editor: Debra A. Stollenwerk
Senior Editorial Assistant: Penny S. Burleson
Production Editor: Kimberly J. Lundy
Production Coordination: Clarinda Publication Services
Design Coordinator: Diane C. Lorenzo
Cover Designer: Ali Mohrman
Cover Image: Linda A. Sorrells Smith
Production Manager: Pamela D. Bennett
Director of Marketing: Kevin Flanagan
Marketing Manager: Krista Groshong
Marketing Services Manager: Barbara Koontz

This book was set in Berkeley Book by The Clarinda Company. It was printed and bound by
R. R. Donnelly & Sons. The cover was printed by Phoenix Color Corp.

Pearson Education Ltd., *London*
Pearson Education Australia Pty. Limited, *Sydney*
Pearson Education Singapore Pte. Ltd.
Pearson Education North Asia Ltd., *Hong Kong*
Pearson Education Canada, Ltd., *Toronto*
Pearson Educación de Mexico, S.A. de C.V.
Pearson Education—Japan, *Tokyo*
Pearson Education Malaysia Pte. Ltd.
Pearson Education, *Upper Saddle River, New Jersey*

Merrill
Prentice Hall

10 9 8 7 6 5 4 3 2 1
ISBN 0-13-031919-8

Preface

Technology is rapidly changing our schools. New interactive learning technologies, particularly the Internet, are altering the 3500-year relationship between teachers and students. These technologies are providing teachers and students with vast and seemingly endless access to learning resources. At the same time, the technologies are a source of novel mediums that allow teachers and students to explore these learning resources together.

Because of these interactive technologies, a new kind of teacher is emerging. The task of teaching is shifting from one of delivering content to students to a new role of providing a context for learning and assisting students in constructing meaning in learning. Today's new interactive technologies are reshaping how and why we learn, and creating a curriculum with rough and porous edges. It is evident that teachers must adjust to these changes.

LearningWebs: Curriculum Journeys on the Internet invites all classroom teachers to join in this momentous evolution by becoming knowledgeable about the new technologies. Unfortunately, it has been estimated that fewer than one-half of all classroom teachers in America currently actively use interactive technologies with their students. Our book is for every teacher interested in entering this new era, but especially for the majority of classroom teachers who feel technologically inadequate or who lack confidence in their ability to use the new technologies to modify the present curriculum.

LearningWebs: Curriculum Journeys on the Internet was written by real teachers for other practicing teachers. It provides a concise and coherent introduction to the power of the Internet to enhance and improve classroom teaching and student learning. This book will show you in easy-to-learn steps how to develop Internet-assisted lessons in your classroom in order to improve student learning.

Thirty years ago, an Austrian named Ivan Illich wrote an important book, *Deschooling Society* (1970). In his book, Illich distinguished between learning that is controlled and constrictive and learning that is natural and expansive. He referred to these two forms of learning as "funnels" and "webs." This was one of the earliest uses of the term *web*, which today is part of everyone's vocabulary (as in World Wide Web, or www).

Illich advocated abandoning the restrictive "funnels" of organized schooling, including highly prescriptive curricula, testing, and preoccupation with credentialing. He sought to develop a new and rich learning environment "in which educational webs heighten the opportunity for each person to transform each moment of his living into one of learning, sharing, and caring."

Illich envisioned "an educational network or web for the autonomous assembly of resources under the control of each learner." He called for an educational system with three purposes: "to provide for all who want access to available resources; to empower those who want to share what they know with those who want to learn from them; and to present an issue with an opportunity to make the (learning) challenge known." He concluded that such learning webs "could spread equal opportunity for learning."

Thirty years have passed, and through the Internet, Illich's ideas about learning webs and the freedom to learn have become feasible. In the past ten years, instant access to persons or resources anywhere on earth has become an operational reality. People can learn, people can teach, people can share, and people can challenge ideas on the World Wide Web or Internet.

The world Internet community is growing exponentially, and 11 million of these regular users are children under age 15. Some children's learning occurs in schools, but much of it does not. Things are changing rapidly. Schools are not the only educational locations in 21st-century America.

The Internet, once the monopoly of the English-speaking world, is becoming global. At the writing of this book, the number of non-English-speaking users is exceeding the number who speak English. This linguistic and cultural trend will continue, and the nature of Internet learning will change daily for the foreseeable future.

Critical to the authors' interest in interactive and distributive learning technologies in schools is the impact these forces are having on curriculum. If a curriculum is a plan or design for learning, what effect will endless and seemingly random Internet sites have on such a plan? How will teachers in the classroom plan, direct, and evaluate learning when they no longer control resource acquisition and distribution? These are pressing questions that all teachers, schools, and districts must address.

As teachers ourselves, we see a bright side to this possible teaching-learning crisis in education. For years, classroom teachers have been subjected to increasing control of what they can and cannot do as the directors of learning. Publishing companies, legislators, and test makers have eroded the teacher's autonomy to make instructional decisions. In some cases today, teaching is a mechanical act. In the words of Illich, a massive "learning funnel" has been created in many of today's schools.

The new interactive technologies, however, provide an opportunity for novel roles and leadership responsibilities for teachers. As increasing numbers of computers with Internet connections reach the classrooms, schools and districts will increasingly depend on classroom teachers to serve as leaders in instructional decision making. Classroom teachers will define and guide learning in the new technological age. And, we believe, such instructional leadership and decision making will be in a highly professional and more artistic capacity, unlike the somewhat mechanical function now experienced by many classroom teachers.

LearningWebs: Curriculum Journeys on the Internet can serve as a possible point of entry for the majority of teachers who are still tentative about their role in using the Internet in the classroom. This text is intended to lead the reader through a basic understanding of computer use in schools, and show the reader some different ways that the Internet can "shape" the school curriculum.

After introducing the reader to the Internet, we identify eight of the most common curriculum designs found in schools and provide sample Internet lessons for each design. Regardless of what your school is doing with curriculum, you can use the Internet to enrich learning for your students.

Finally, we show you how to create a "curriculum journey" for your own classroom. Resource E focuses on 240 common school topics, K–12, and provides 1,200 safe sites that the authors have screened for your use. This screening is especially important today, given the lack of quality control agents on the Internet and the growing problem of pornography hidden behind innocuous-sounding titles.

Since ours is a text for the new technology, we direct you to the Companion Website for this book; see **http://www.prenhall.com/keating**.

Using all of these tools, we set you free as one of the growing membership of teachers with the technical skills to be successful in the 21st-century classroom.

—*The Authors*

Discover the Companion Website Accompanying This Book

THE PRENTICE HALL COMPANION WEBSITE: A VIRTUAL LEARNING ENVIRONMENT

Technology is a constantly growing and changing aspect of our field that is creating a need for content and resources. To address this emerging need, Prentice Hall has developed an online learning environment for students and professors alike—Companion Websites—to support our textbooks.

In creating a Companion Website, our goal is to build on and enhance what the textbook already offers. For this reason, the content for each user-friendly website is organized by topic and provides the professor and student with a variety of meaningful resources. Common features of a Companion Website include:

FOR THE INSTRUCTOR

Every Companion Website integrates **Syllabus Manager™**, an online syllabus creation and management utility.

- **Syllabus Manager™** provides you, the instructor, with an easy, step-by-step process to create and revise syllabi, with direct links into Companion Website and other online content without having to learn HTML.

- Students may log on to your syllabus during any study session. All they need to know is the web address for the Companion Website and the password you've assigned to your syllabus.

- After you have created a syllabus using **Syllabus Manager™**, students may enter the syllabus for their course section from any point in the Companion Website.

- Clicking on a date, the student is shown the list of activities for the assignment. The activities for each assignment are linked directly to actual content, saving time for students.

- Adding assignments consists of clicking on the desired due date, then filling in the details of the assignment—name of the assignment, instructions, and whether or not it is a one-time or repeating assignment.

- In addition, links to other activities can be created easily. If the activity is online, a URL can be entered in the space provided, and it will be linked automatically in the final syllabus.

- Your completed syllabus is hosted on our servers, allowing convenient up-dates from any computer on the Internet. Changes you make to your syllabus are immediately available to your students at their next logon.

FOR THE STUDENT

The Companion Website includes many features that support and expand upon classroom lessons.

- **Topic Overviews** outline key concepts in topic areas
- **Web Links** provide a wide range of websites that provide useful and current information related to each topic area
- **Lesson Plans** offer links to topic-specific lesson plans
- **Professional Development**—links to all pertinent associations and organizations in the field, in addition to web-based professional development materials
- **Standards** outline general technology standards in addition to technology standards for specifc content areas of teaching
- **Teacher's Toolbox**—useful Web-based resources for teachers, including Software & Web Site Reviews, Computer Basics, Technology Grants, and Technology Classrooms
- **Electronic Bluebook**—send homework or essays directly to your instructor's email with this paperless form
- **Message Board**—serves as a virtual bulletin board to post—or respond to—questions or comments to/from a national audience
- **Chat**—real-time chat with anyone who is using the text anywhere in the country—ideal for discussion and study groups, class projects, etc.

To take advantage of these and other resources, please visit the Companion Website to accompany *LearningWebs: Curriculum Journeys on the Internet* at

www.prenhall.com/keating

About the Authors

The authors are practicing educators in northeast Florida. Michele Keating is a fifth-grade teacher at R. B. Hunt Elementary School in St. Augustine, Florida. She has won numerous awards for teaching in math, science, and special education and serves as the technical specialist in her school. Michele is a member of the prestigous Florida League of Teachers.

Jon Wiles is a professor of education at the University of North Florida in Jacksonville. The author of twelve major texts in the area of teaching and educational leadership, Jon is currently focused on Internet-assisted curriculum.

Mary Wood Piazza is an English teacher at Palatka High School in Palatka, Florida and is the designer of the LearningWebs Internet site (*http.//www.learnweb.org*).

The authors are co-directors of a nonprofit Florida corporation, LearningWebs, Inc., dedicated to assisting teachers entering the new technological age in schools.

Contents

NOTE: Every effort has been made to provide accurate and current Internet information in this book. However, the Internet and information posted on it are constantly changing, so it is inevitable that some of the Internet addresses listed in this textbook will change.

CHAPTER 1

Understanding the Internet

Upon this gifted age
in its darkest hour
Rains from the sky
A meteoric shower of facts
They lie unquestioned
Uncombined
Wisdom enough to leech us from our ill
It is spun daily
Yet there exists no loom
To weave it into fabric

Edna St. Vincent Millay

This is a book for teachers who are undecided or unsure about how to integrate computers and the Internet into their curriculum. Various sources tell us that the majority of all classroom teachers do *not* use the new interactive technologies in their teaching. This is a cause for concern because nearly all schools in America now have computers, and most are adding Internet connections as quickly as possible. In addition, 11 million children and youth now have access to the Internet, and Internet usage in the United States is doubling every 100 days.

The computer industry is one of the fastest-growing industries in history; technology advancements double every 18 months. According to Gordon Moore of Intel (who derived Moore's Law), computer technology could grow 100 times more powerful within a decade. By 2005, one billion people will be connected to the Internet, and they will speak many languages and represent many cultures. These statistics, and their implication for education, are staggering.

The authors of this book are teachers and, therefore, busy people like yourself. We all know intuitively that something momentous is happening to teaching and learning, but it is hard to put a finger on exactly what that something might be. After all, we've had computers in schools for nearly two decades, and more are added all the time. Maybe, we think, we can just keep doing what we've always done and this will all go away, but in fact, this will not happen. These new learning technologies represent either a threat or an opportunity for teachers, depending on how we view them.

We, the authors, believe that the emerging new interactive technologies represent an opportunity for classroom teachers to reestablish a leadership role in instruction. We think that the millions of Internet sites are a treasure trove for learning and that classroom teachers can most effectively manage these new learning tools in the classroom. No publishing company, no university, no school district, and no state department of education can monitor or control the changes in school curriculum that are beginning to occur as the Internet reaches into the classroom. In our opinion, classroom teachers will be the instructional leaders in this new era of learning in schools.

WHAT IS THE INTERNET?

Do you remember when computers first appeared in schools in the 1980s? They were pretty simple machines with limited memory, and very little software was available. We used them for drill practice and entertainment. Soon, Apple Computer established itself as the "teacher's company" and its Apple IIe became the classroom standard. Within a few years, we had computer labs in schools, and even some in-school networks (LAN—local area networks). The sophisticated districts linked schools together in multischool networks (WAN–wide area networks). There still wasn't much change in the delivery of instruction, and teachers saw these machines as supplements at best.

Outside of schools, computers were having much greater impact. In 1969, the U.S. military linked military sites together through something called ARPAnet (the Advanced Research Project Agency net). Then, in 1986, the National Science Foundation Network (NSFNET) was constructed by the federal government as a noncommercial network of six supercomputer sites. Finally, on April 30, 1995, most of the functions of NSFNET were made available for, or were replaced by, commercial services and the modern Internet was born. This "network of networks" connects computers across the world in one gigantic global communication system known as the World Wide Web (www).

The World Wide Web, or just "the Web," allows the sharing of information from one location to any other location almost instantly. The various connected networks are owned and maintained by research, commercial, educational, and governmental organizations. Anyone with the appropriate software and user access can post information on the Web; this is both good and bad news. The good news is that the modern Web is the richest information source ever developed. The bad news is that some of the information is not accurate, some is purposefully deceptive, and some is inappropriate for students. Every day in schools, teachers are the final filter, differentiating what constitutes valuable knowledge and what does not.

The most important thing to understand at this point is that you don't have to be a "techie" to use the Internet effectively today. All you need is the determination to learn to employ this great tool and the skill of pointing and clicking with your trackball, mouse, or keypad. We are going to share with you how to use this tool in your classroom so you can begin to take advantage of its amazing learning opportunities for you and your students.

You will need software that allows you to view and download information from the Web. Netscape Navigator and Microsoft Explorer, two of the most popular Web browsers, make it easy for teachers and students to travel the Web. Hypertext is used by these browsers to create a multimedia environment in which print, video, and sound are combined on web pages. (The "http" in an Internet address stands for *hypertext transport protocol*). Another important feature of hypertext is that it allows for nonlinear access of information, which encourages exploration and natural learning.

Together, the World Wide Web (www) part of the Internet, browsers, search engines, and websites comprise what is known as the ISDN, or the Integrated Services Digital Network.

WILL THE INTERNET REALLY CHANGE TEACHING?

The careers of most classroom teachers have been characterized by an almost endless stream of innovations, fads, and gadgets passing through America's single biggest consumer market. This year's technology or curriculum bromide is often next year's trash. Teachers are discouraged by superfluous change for its own sake. Believe us, we've been there!

There is nothing new about teachers using media, for we've been using all kinds of media throughout our careers. When teachers used media in the past, however, such use was severely restricted by the fact that the teacher was the sole activating agent of that media. We turned it on and turned it off, and we decided what the student would or would not see or experience. The critical difference is, the new media (the Internet) is not teacher dependent, at least not at present.

This, of course, calls into question the role teachers will play. For the moment, though, focus on the exciting fact that each student can have a unique learning experience using this new media. Haven't we been struggling to meet the needs of all learners in the classroom? It is only logical that teachers who attempt to control and standardize all learning will experience frustration, a loss of authority, and perhaps even a decline in self-esteem when the Internet becomes a fixture in their classrooms.

The world of classroom learning is leaving behind the pattern of total teacher control of the last 3,500 years and moving toward a new type of learning that will be collaborative, exploratory, multimedia, multisensory, authentic, and student directed. In reality, such change is already occurring as some teachers accept their new role and embrace the evolving face of education. Others are still waiting to see if this most recent change is genuine.

The National Educational Technology Standards Group at *http://cnets.iste.org/condition.htm* contrasts the traditional and new ways of learning in the manner, as shown in Figure 1.1.

Because of the computer, but especially because of the Internet, education is changing. Student learning is becoming increasingly individualized, personalized, exploratory, and collaborative. The use of the Internet in the classroom develops and

Traditional Learning Environments ⟶	New Learning Environments
Teacher-centered instruction	Student-centered learning
Single sense stimulation	Multisensory stimulation
Single path progression	Multipath progression
Single media	Multimedia
Isolated work	Collaborative work
Information delivered	Information exchange
Passive learning	Active/exploratory/ inquiry-based learning
Factual, knowledge-based learning	Critical thinking and informed decision-making
Reactive response	Pro-active/planned action
Isolated, artificial context	Authentic, real-world context

Figure 1.1   Establishing New Learning Environments: Incorporating New Strategies

enhances learner creativity. Teaching is becoming more personal and artistic, and it is up to the classroom teacher to define this new way of learning.

SOME SAMPLE CHANGES POSSIBLE

We would like to highlight eight kinds of instructional opportunities that are presently emerging in America's classrooms because of the new interactive technologies. These are changes that can impact your classroom right away, and you'll learn about some of these topics in this book.

1. Teachers, students, and parents will communicate using electronic mail (e-mail); this will encourage additional learning at home and better communication about what's happening at school.
2. Regular classroom instruction will be supplemented by Internet sites of infinite variety and richness. Literally, the world's resources will be at teachers' fingertips.
3. Teachers can begin to individualize learning experiences for students by creating curriculum journeys. Resource E in this book will present the reader with a starter set of 240 common K–12 topics (1,200 sites) useful for building such learning journeys.
4. The Internet can serve as a source of rewards or motivation. Kids can visit the Disney site, go to Legoland, and learn about things they enjoy such as dinosaurs and volcanoes.
5. Teachers can create interdisciplinary sites where various subjects and knowledge can be applied to problem areas or areas of interest.
6. Children can gain perspective and experience by taking electronic field trips to places such as Yosemite Park or the Louvre in Paris. These "virtual trips" can serve as background for regular classroom learning.
7. Free exploration of a chosen topic using Internet search engines can capture students' imaginations and encourage in-depth learning.
8. The Internet is a useful vehicle for the acquisition and practice of basic skills and provides opportunities for the development of critical and creative thinking skills.

In conclusion, there is a dynamic change occuring in classroom instruction and in learning, wherever it occurs. The Internet presents teachers with an opportunity to regain a leadership role in curriculum development and delivery. Teachers in the United States have been guarded in their acceptance of the new interactive technologies and Internet use, but they must get "on board" if they are to remain effective with their technology-savvy students in the 21st century. The opportunities presented by this development far outweigh the challenges of learning to navigate on the Web.

In the next chapter, we will check on the best vehicles for our "journey," we will learn how to navigate the information highway, and we will visit some sites of interest to educators. Let's get moving!

READINGS

American Psychological Association. *Learner-centered principles: A framework for school redesign and reform 1997*. http://www.apa.org/ed/lep.html.

Coley, R. (1997). *Computers in the classroom: The status of technology in U.S. schools.* Princeton, N.J.: Educational Testing Service.

National Center for Educational Statistics. *Teacher use of computers and the Internet in public schools.* http://nces.ed.gov/spider/webspider/2000090.shtml.

National School Boards Association. *Present and future change: Technology and learning, 1997.* www.nsba.org.

SELECTED LEARNING ACTIVITIES

1. Visit the Web page *Essential Conditions to Make It Happen* on the website for the National Educational Technology Standards, (*http://cnets.iste.org/condition.htm*), and read the rationale for changes from traditional ways of learning (as listed in Figure 1.1). Compare this rationale to the eight changes projected in this chapter.

2. The National Educational Technology Standards Group contrasts traditional and new ways of learning in the classroom of the future. Write a short essay on your reaction to these changes, identifying those you feel are most important.

3. Visit the Companion Website for this book at *www.prenhall.com/keating/*. Report what you find at this site.

Exploring the Internet

*I am convinced that it is of primordial
importance to learn more each year
than the year before.
After all, what is education but a process
by which a person begins how to learn
to learn.*

Peter Ustinov

Don't worry, seat belts are not necessary for this journey through the Web! It will be exciting, but there is no danger involved. To travel the Internet, you will need a computer, an Internet account, a gateway, and browser software. The Internet, a network of networks, is similar to a system of roads and highways webbing or connecting the world. To access it, you will need a ramp or entryway to the World Wide Web. This access ramp will be provided by a private commercial account or through your school or state educational server. To set up a personal Internet account, contact a commercial service provider for home Internet use, or your school technology coordinator for school use. National providers include AT&T, America Online, Bell South, GEnie, Prodigy, and EarthLink. To obtain information on regional Internet providers, visit the Providers of Commercial Internet Access site at *http://www.celestin.com.*

A "gateway" is simply your computer's connection to the Internet. It can be a modem and phone line at home, a network cable plugged into your school's network ports, or simply wireless access using an airport. Once you have a computer, a modem or network connection, an Internet account, and a browser, the toughest part is over. The rest of this journey will be a fun exploration of the Internet. You can do this, you will do this, and you will be forever changed as a teacher and a learner!

JOURNEYS USING WEB ADDRESSES (URLS)

Once you've logged on to the Internet, you will need to make some travel plans. Locations to visit on the "Web" are generally called web sites. Specific locations are called "web pages," and the cover page for any web page is the "home page." To locate any person or resource in the world on the Internet, you will need to know an address, location, or site.

When exploring the Internet, the same is true. Whether you use Netscape Navigator or Microsoft® Explorer, an address box located across the top of the Web page displays the designated location, address, or Web site. The same box may be labeled "URL"; this stands for Uniform Resource Locator, another name which means "Internet address." A picture of this address box, using Netscape, is shown below, and the address displayed, *http://www.learnweb.org,* is Learningwebs, our Web site.

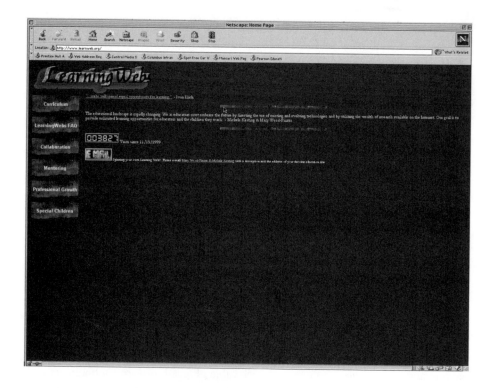

As you use this book, you'll get plenty of practice in using web addresses. A note of caution is in order regarding web addresses: since most of these addresses are case sensitive, when entering an address you must type that address *exactly as you see it.* You can't substitute capitals for lowercase, respell words, or add or delete spaces that appear inappropriate. Many of these addresses seem strange and use confusing abbreviations. Your browser, like a mail carrier, cannot locate an incorrect or incomplete address. Let's practice using an address to reach a desired destination.

1. Click on the address box on your computer screen. It will probably turn a color such as dark blue if there was already an address there.
2. Now you can type right over that address.

3. Type in the address *http://www.learnweb.org/* and then hit the Return key on your keyboard. If you were successful, in a few seconds, you should see this picture on your screen.

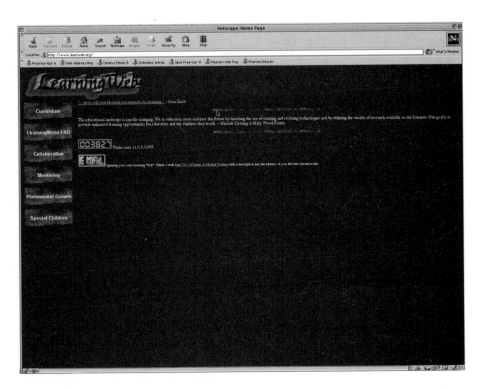

Bookmarks

When you discover a site that you want to visit frequently, your browser makes it easy to remember the address. In Netscape, simply click on the Bookmark menu above the words Netscape:Home page, and select or click on "Add a Bookmark." If you are using Microsoft Explorer software, click on the Favorites menu and select "Add a Favorite."

Let's give it a try!

1. With LearningWebs still on the screen, go to the Bookmarks or Favorites Menu, and add this site.
2. Now, click on Bookmarks or Favorites again, scroll to the last entry, and see if it is LearningWebs. If so, great! You've done it! There's your first bookmark.
3. To return to this site at another time, simply click on Bookmarks or Favorites, scroll to the site you'd like to revisit, and when it is highlighted, release the mouse button.

Search Engines

The second and less direct, but more interesting, route to Internet travel involves search engines. For some, this name conjures up visions of a big metal apparatus with gears cranking out lists of web sites. In (virtual) reality, search engines are commercial web sites that will help you find other sites on the Web. They also will show you some advertisements; this is how they provide the service.

Search engines operate in two basic ways. Spider-based engines electronically visit web sites and index them into huge catalogs. Examples of this type are Webcrawler, *http://www.webcrawler.com,* and Altavista, *http://www.altavista.com.* If you prefer a human touch, try directory-based services such as Yahoo *http://www.yahoo.com,* or Galaxy, *http://www.galaxy.com.* Information on these engines is organized by subjects and compiled by humans.

Other popular search engines you may wish to try include:

Hotbot
http://www.hotbot.com
provides many options for defining searches

Northern Lights
http://www.northernlight.com
searches by broad topics

Mamma
http://www.mamma.com
runs multiple search engines

Dogpile
http://www.dogpile.com
runs multiple search engines

Internet Sleuth
http:// internetsleuth.com
runs multiple search engines

Metacrawler
http://www.metacrawler.com
conducts simultaneous searches with five search engines

Ask Jeeves
http://www.askjeeves.com
searches in question format

Excite
http://www.excite.com
a summary of sites

Creative names, aren't they? Let's try a category search using Yahoo, one of the most widely used search engines. Suppose you want to know more about searching the Internet.

1. Type the Yahoo address *http://www. yahoo.com* in the address box and hit the Return key. When you've reached the Yahoo home page, you will see many categories listed. Sometimes you have to scroll down a bit because of all the ads.
2. Click on the line that reads "Computers and Internet."
3. On the next page you'll find some subcategories of "Computers & Internet"; choose "World Wide Web."
4. Next, choose "Searching the Web."
5. Now click on "How to Search the Web."
6. Try the site named "How to Search the World Wide Web: A Tutorial and Guide for Beginners" or any other site that looks interesting to you.

You have just completed a search by category! Be sure to use Bookmark or select Favorite for any site you may wish to revisit later. The technique is to start with a general topic and get more and more specific. You are on your way to becoming a search expert!

Keyword Searches

Now that you are an experienced web traveler, let's try a keyword search. Suppose you'd like to visit a fabulous art museum. Let's use the Yahoo search engine again. You might begin by typing in the word "museum" in the search text box and then clicking Search. If you've got time to visit several hundred museums on-line, go for it! If not, you may want to narrow your topic a bit. If you are interested in museums in France, for example, try typing "French Museums" or "museums of France" in the Search text box. This should significantly limit the number of topics. It is important to be as specific as possible, even if you don't know exactly where you are going.

If you are searching with a spider-based search engine, such as Alta Vista, put the words in quotation marks (" ") to list an exact phrase. If you are searching for a site dealing with civil rights in the United States, with quotation marks around the phrase you'll get only links related to that topic. Without the marks, hundreds of sites may be listed: every site with *civil, rights, movement,* or *United States* in it.

We have found that student use of search engines encourages exploration, non-linear learning, and self-directed learning. Searching leads to those off-the-main-road side trips where often the most relevant and high-level thinking and learning take place. Occasionally, a web explorer may find herself at an unplanned destination, which results in great pleasure and inspiration. This is a very important point for classroom teachers to note.

As you search using specific addresses or by topic using search engines, be sure to bookmark valuable sites to which you'd like instant access in the future. If you ever feel "lost in cyberspace," fear not. Use the Back button on your browser to shift your journey into reverse. Or, click the Home button to return to your preset home web site, and put yourself into motion again using the Forward button.

USEFUL SITES FOR TEACHERS

A staggering number of new web sites appear on the Internet each day. For example, in the first six months of the year 2000, over five million new web sites were added to the Internet. Don't be overwhelmed by the many choices; you have already earned your learner's permit, and you are ready to try a little cruising on your own. As you travel the "information superhighway," you will notice that often there are brightly colored words in the text. These are the HyperText protocol (http) "links" mentioned in Chapter 1. While at a web site, you can click on one of these links with your mouse, and you'll be on the road to a related site. To get back to where you were, click on the Back button.

We close this chapter with a few web sites that you, as a teacher, may find helpful and interesting as you become an expert Internet traveler. A complete list of useful teacher sites is found in Resource A of this book.

Teacher Sites

Learning Webs
http://www.learnweb.org
This site was developed by teachers for teachers, with links to curriculum, professional development, training, collaboration, and special children's resources. It also provides sample learning webs from real schools in the United States.

Tappedin
http://www.tappedin.org
This is a cybercampus where teachers can share resources, collaborate, hold real-time meetings, and meet new colleagues from around the world.

21st-Century Teachers Network
http://www.21ct.org
This site assists teachers in the integration of technology into the curriculum to improve student learning.

Teacher/Pathfinder
http://teacherpathfinder.org
This is an educational Internet village where you can find hundreds of links related to professional development, curriculum, assessment, community involvement, and parental involvement.

TeacherVision
http://www. teachervision.com/index.html
This site provides a reference desk with on-line reference materials, downloadable software, class web pages, graphic organizers, and lots of great resources for teachers.

Kathy Schrock's Guide for Educators
http://school.discovery.com/schrockguide
This site is one of the oldest and best resource links for teachers.

On-Line Internet Lessons

The Help Web
http://www.imaginarylandscape.com/helpweb/welcome.html
This is a guide to getting started on the Internet.

Internet 101
http://www2.famvid.com/i101/internet101.html
This site provides an excellent tutorial for Internet beginners.

Web Teacher
http://www.webteacher.org/macnet/indextc.html
This web primer covers topics from browsers to newsgroups.

Research and Reference Tools

The *Kappan*
http://www.pdkintl.org
This is the monthly journal of Phi Delta Kappa International.

Educational Leadership
http://www.ascd.org
This site provides research and articles from the monthly journal of the Association for Supervision and Curriculum Development.

On-Line Dictionaries
http://facstaff.bucknell.edu/rbeard/diction.html
This site links users to reference materials and dictionaries.

National Geographic Maps
http://www.nationalgeographic.com/resources/ngo/maps
This site provides political, physical, and virtual maps searchable by region or country.

Searchopolis
http://www.searchopolis.com
This is a site with links to many reference tools.

For Students

Yahooligans
http://www.yahooligans.com
This is the kids' own version of Yahoo.

Ask Jeeves for Kids
http://www.ajkids.com
Students can conduct research at this site by posing questions.

By now you are probably feeling pretty comfortable and confident. Let's move on to Chapter 3 and determine how these resources can make you a better classroom teacher and enrich your existing curriculum.

READINGS

Becker, H. (1999). *Teaching, learning, and computing 1998: A national survey of schools and teachers.* Irvine, Calif.: University of California.

CEO Forum on Education and Technology, *http://www.ceoforum.org.*

Jostens Learning Education Forum, *Jessica's Generation: Learning, Technology, and the Future of K–12 Education,* 1995.

Tapscott, Dan. *Growing up digital: The rise of the Net generation.* New York: McGraw-Hill, 1997.

SELECTED LEARNING ACTIVITIES

1. Take a few minutes to browse through the authors' web page, LearningWebs, at *www.learnweb.org.* How is it organized? Would you like to make suggestions for new items? E-mail the authors.
2. This chapter lists various educational resources for teachers. Take an hour and browse through three or four of these. Which are most useful? Why?
3. There are many search engines on the Internet. Why do you suppose Yahoo is the most frequently used search engine?

CHAPTER 3

How the Internet Fits Classroom Lessons

It is nothing short of a miracle
that the modern methods of
instruction have not yet entirely
strangled the holy curiosity of inquiry.
Albert Einstein

By now you should be feeling pretty confident that that you can get onto and use the Internet. After all, it is really just a matter of pointing and clicking the mouse until you arrive at a desired destination. The Internet is so rich and intriguing; your curiosity just keeps taking you further and further into the intricate web of sites.

Once the novelty of exploring wears off, you will begin to address the question of how this learning tool can make you a better classroom teacher. We often hear fellow teachers say things such as, "This is great but we are really focused on basic skills and standards testing at our school. . . . I just don't have time for this."

We, the authors, believe we must view and evaluate Internet use in the classroom in terms of the specific goals or objectives that we hold for our students. These projected results might include statements such as:

"We want our students to know the facts."

"We want our students to have the skills."

"We want our students to understand."

"We want our students to be able to work together."

"We want our students to use this in the real world."

"We want our students to love to learn."

These are all valuable goals for teachers to strive for, and the Internet can assist teachers in reaching these goals for their students. A point of origin in thinking about the Internet in the classroom is to "see" the organization or design of the school curriculum. A curriculum is a plan for promoting learning. Each school and each classroom tends to value and emphasize some things over others; there are always priorities.

In schools, teachers use various phrases to describe different curriculum designs. We'll say we are emphasizing basic skills, or that we have an interdisciplinary approach to instruction, or that we feature cooperative learning in our classrooms. The authors know, from experience, that the Internet can be used to enhance and support any design for learning found in today's schools. In fact, in Chapter 4 of this book, we will provide you with Internet lessons adapted to eight common curriculum designs and teach you how to create such lessons in your classroom regardless of your school's philosophy or the mission of your curriculum.

EIGHT CURRICULUM DESIGNS

At least eight types of curriculum designs are common in schools in the United States. Figure 3.1 is an overview of these eight designs organized to reflect their increasing complexity, from the more basic Content-Based curriculum through Critical/Creative Thinking, the most complex design. Each design represents a vision of what the school is trying to help the student learn. Most schools have a blended curriculum with multiple purposes, but many lessons in the classroom have a single learning objective. Teachers tailor the curriculum for individual needs to develop classroom lessons.

Type	Purpose	Activity
Critical/Creative Thinking	Construction of new knowledge and forms	Model-building Free imagination
Problem-Solving	Issues analysis Skills application	Current events Futurism
Cooperative Learning	Social skill development Shared decision-making	Cooperative activity Group work
Interdisciplinary	Connecting information	Organizing, ordering
Conceptual Learning	Understanding	Big ideas, familiarity
Inquiry Approach	Awareness, interest	Stories, unknowns
Skill-Based Instruction	Manipulation, patterns	Rules, practice, ordering
Content-Based	Knowledge acquisition	Facts, representative form

Figure 3.1   Eight Common Curriculum Designs

Note Reprinted, by permission of the publisher, from Wiles, J. & Bondi, J. (2002). *Curriculum development: A guide to practice* (6th ed.). Upper Saddle River, NJ: Merrill/Prentice Hall.

Content-Based Curriculum

Most schools teach from a content-based curriculum which identifies information to be learned each year; it is generally organized as a study discipline. Lessons in such a curriculum would consist of facts, data, and information representative of all knowledge in that area. Acquiring this formal knowledge, which is perceived as the basis of education in our society, is the purpose of classroom instruction.

The Internet contains a vast number of sites that address topical knowledge. For example, if you go to any search engine previously mentioned and type in the keywords "quadratic equations," you will find over 10,000 sites addressing this topic alone. You may wish to check five of these sites as part of your curriculum journeys in Chapter 4. When searching by category, begin your search with "math." Then narrow your search to "quadratic equations."

Two content-based sites worth mentioning are:

Free Federal Resources for Educational Excellence
http://www.ed.gov/free
Choose your subject area, and this site will provide you with links to all kinds of resources, such as how to help your child learn math.

Yahoo Education
http://dir.yahoo.com/Education/k_12
Choose your subject, and use a category search to descend into more and more detail, such as Social Studies/history/archaeology/lesson plans/pictures.

Skills-Based Curriculum

There is hardly a school district in the United States today that isn't testing, testing, testing for basic skills. The standards-based era is upon us, and classroom teachers are under significant pressure to produce test score gains that show student mastery of basic skills. The Internet is a great resource for this type of teaching.

The skills taught in schools are of two types. First, there are repetitive manipulations, such as the operations in math or learning to spell. In these cases, practice makes perfect. The second type of skills-based curriculum addresses sequencing and patterns. Learning the "scientific method" is an example of this type. The Internet is loaded with help sites in this category. Some of our favorites are:

The Worksheet Factory
http://www.worksheetfactory.com
Pull down and print these practice sheets.

Breakthrough to Literacy
http://www.wrightgroup.com
This site offers skills-based lessons.

Math Connections
http://www.mathconnections.com
Skills-based secondary mathematics curriculum are offered at this site, along with professional development workshops.

Florida Department of Education
http://www.sunshinestatestandards.net
Florida's Sunshine State Standards are the model of skills-based learning. This site contains standards, lesson plans, and a host of tools.

Bluweb'n
http://www.kn.pacbell.com/wired/bluewebn
This is a great source of teacher-made lesson plans, many addressing basic skills mastery.

Inquiry and Exploratory Curriculum

Children are naturally inquisitive. Put a student in front of a computer with Internet access and that student is in his or her element. Any topic can be found and explored on-line. But how does this natural learning fit into the planned experiences of formal schooling? The authors believe that the word *motivation* identifies the connection.

Learning theories differ on whether an idea should be introduced before the facts (deductive) or whether the factual learning should come before the generalization (inductive). Regardless of where curiosity fits in the scheme of things, classroom teachers know that motivation is an essential ingredient for classroom learning.

The Internet can help develop interest and motivation in students. The search for unknowns, or simply exploring stories that hint at the uses of knowledge, contributes to motivation. The following are some sites that we like:

Books for Beginning and Early Independent Readers
http://www.geocities.com/teachingwithheart/levelbooks.html
This provides links to quality books for independent readers selected by librarians.

Global Access to Educational Sources
http://www.athena.ivv.nasa.gov/
This site, with hundreds of links to independent learning, is for middle school students.

Independence High School
http://www2.umdnj.edu/chinjweb/independentlearning.htm
The Washington State site provides opportunities for independent exploration.

Center for Independent Learning
http://intergate.sdmesa.sdccd.cc.ca.us/home/home.html
This site provides over 100 learning programs to students who are self-motivated.

French Government Tourist Office of the United States.
http://www.francetourism.com
Simply send your student on a prelesson journey. Paris, anyone?

Conceptual Curriculum

Many school lessons are designed to increase student understanding of complex topics. Rather than focus on the individual components, these lessons look at the "big picture" or seek to introduce an idea to students. What is prejudice? How can airplanes fly? What constitutes pollution?

Global in its orientation, conceptual learning uses a wide-angle lens to view the world. Internet resources are perfectly adapted to this kind of teaching and learning. Here are several sites that are useful if conceptual development is the focus of your curriculum:

Teaching Science Conceptually
http://www.athena.ivv.nasa.gov
This site defines concept teaching and leads teachers to resources that support this kind of instruction.

The Powerposse

http://powerposse.apsc.com

At this site, four experienced teachers show what a concept lesson is like in various subjects and at each grade level.

We also direct the reader to the sites in the journey activity "Flight" in Chapter 4 as an example of teaching a complex conceptual idea to elementary school students.

Interdisciplinary Curriculum

For years, interdisciplinary instruction has been a trademark of middle schools. For the special learners who attend middle schools, "pulling thoughts together" is an important task. As they transition through puberty, all of their knowledge and reference points are realigned. Interdisciplinary teaching seeks to show the various connections between school and the real world in which we all live. It attempts to make learning purposeful, often using an applied or "hands-on" methodology.

The Internet is a good resource for developing interdisciplinary units, providing colorful, relevant, and lively topics for students to organize and order. Two sites that will introduce the utility of the Internet are:

The Battle of Vicksburg

http://www.nps.gov/vick

An understanding of the issues of the Civil War are greatly enhanced by this U.S. Park Service site. Various subject areas (math, language arts, science, social studies, and art) are integrated to explain how and why this famous battle occurred.

Webquest

http://.edweb.sdsu.edu/webquest/taskonomy.html

Using common subject matter, this creative site provides ready-made learning tasks such as retelling, compiling, designing, product creation, analysis, and judgment to understand a topic area.

Cooperative Learning Curriculum

During the last decade, many teachers have tried to use cooperative learning methods in their classrooms. Research studies and teacher experiences tell us that this is a valuable way to teach. Cooperative learning strategies produce achievement and also encourage student interaction and the development of shared decision-making skills.

The Internet is a very useful tool for a teacher employing this instructional pattern in the classroom. As an introduction to this resource we suggest the following sites:

1. For a discussion of the techniques and various models of cooperative learning, visit this site.
   http://www.mariposa.k12.ca.us
2. Find resources and readings in the application of the Internet to cooperative learning programs at this site.
   http://www.kagancooplearn.com

3. Look for planning guidelines, documents, materials, activities, and technological adaptations here.
   http://doe.concordia.ca/cslp

Problem-Solving Curriculum

In many subjects, the application of acquired knowledge is a lesson goal. Students can learn to apply skills and make assessments of conditions in society. Current events and the future are natural topic areas for such learning.

Because the Internet has so many topical sites, it provides a rich resource for teachers exploring issues and the application of subject matter to everyday problems. The authors recommend the following sample Internet sites:

Future Problem Solving
http://fpsp.org/
Paul Torrance, widely acclaimed as a curriculum developer for creative thinking and problem-solving has an exciting web page. His Mars colonization activity is especially good.

21st Century Problem Solving
http:/www2.hawaii.edu/suremath/home.html
For problem-solving in subject areas and a chance to contribute your own activities for others to use, see this site.

Critical and Creative Thinking Curriculum

Many teachers emphasize higher-level thinking skills in their subject areas, and the Internet has many sites to make your classes more exciting.

Critical and creative thinking, although not the same skills, both encourage the creation of new knowledge forms and the development of imagination in students. Some of our favorite sites are suggested for your initial viewing:

Mindbloom
http://www.amiktech.com
Creative thinking techniques are taught here.

Critical Thinking, Inc.
http://www.tools2learn.com/index.html
This University of Rochester site has teacher tools for promoting critical thinking.

The Critical Thinking Place
http://www.criticalthinking.org
Primary and secondary lessons are provided.

In conclusion, there is no question that teachers must see how the Internet can contribute to classroom teaching before they will attempt to use it in developing lessons. We have introduced eight common curriculum designs and communicated our belief that the Internet is a powerful resource for any or all of them.

S. ROBERTSON
+ 2000

In the next chapter, we present techniques for creating Internet-assisted lessons in your classroom. We also refer you to Resource E for 1,200 Internet sites which have been screened and selected for their educational value.

We will show you how, using the 1,200 sites and others that you find, you can construct Internet-assisted lessons. We will provide lessons for each of the eight curriculum designs and provide notes which explain how to build curriculum journeys for your students.

READINGS

Bransford, John (1999). *How people learn: Brain, mind, experience, and school.* Washington: Commission on Behavioral Sciences and Education.

Illich, Ivan (1971). *Deschooling society.* New York: Harper and Row.

North Central Regional Education Laboratory. The curriculum, assessment, and instruction. *http://www.ncrel.org/info/curriculum.*

Wiles, Jon & Bondi, Joseph (2002). *Curriculum development: A guide to practice* (6th ed.). Upper Saddle River, NJ: Merrill/Prentice Hall.

SELECTED LEARNING ACTIVITIES

1. From the readings in the eight curriculum designs section (Figure 3.1), select two designs and review the suggested resources for developing curriculum materials.

2. How does an exploratory curriculum design differ from that of a conceptual design? What can the teacher do to facilitate either design?

CHAPTER 4

Applications and Ownership

In times of dramatic change, it is the learner
who inherits the future. The learned usually
find themselves equipped to live in a world
that no longer exists.

Eric Hoffer

We now have all of the components necessary for creating curriculum journeys across the Internet. We can steer our computer by searching, selecting, saving, and activating sites. Our searches can be keyword or generic, and we isolate our best sites for students into topical webs. We have seen that these Internet lessons will "fit" any curriculum, and we have outlined eight types or designs and identified places to look for further information. Now, we are ready for the process of applying this information and then creating our own curriculum journeys on the Internet.

CREATING LESSONS

When we create a lesson, whatever the design, we usually have some basic components. First, we have the content or "stuff" with which we want the student to interact. This material can be a set of skills, an idea, specific knowledge, or even an unknown.

Second, we usually have an outcome or terminal goal for the lesson. What is it we want the student to be able to do when finished? Third, we usually organize any lesson to emphasize one part over some other part. This is where the design of the curriculum comes into play. Finally, we order our lessons.

A standard classroom lesson has a beginning, a body, and an end. More specifically, the teacher enters the room, introduces the topic, outlines the learning path, commences teaching, and summarizes the lesson on completion. The teacher may or may not provide the "big idea" to the student at first, depending on his or her learning strategy.

This is a complicated way to state that each design and each classroom lesson is organized in a unique manner depending on what they are trying to accomplish. The authors offer a "template" for planning lessons (Figure 4.1). Let's walk through one such lesson, "First Kid in Space."

Planning a Curriculum Journey on the Internet

Imagine yourself a fourth-grade teacher who is about to teach a lesson on physical science to her students. The content of this unit, "Outer Space," will be such things as planets, astronomy, space travel, satellites, and the first landing by man on the moon. While all of these topics are of interest, you must first get the attention of your students and motivate them for more formal learning in the future.

You may decide to create a story about space travel that will introduce students to some of the above topics. This early lesson will be to explore the topics, not master them, and the student will be involved in inquiry learning. The teacher will establish a path of Internet sites for the student that will include such ideas as space camp, the United States Space Center, the Discovery mission, the Hubble telescope, and an introduction to planets. The lesson could be called, "First Kid in Space," and the student who interacts with this lesson will be the star of the show.

You go to your bank of school topics and related Internet sites, and choose some, such as Kennedy Space Center, Hubble telescope, and planets. From these and other topics you select Internet websites. Having done this, you write a script about the first kid in space and place websites in the text to enrich the story. It might read something like the following example.

Sample Journey — First Kid In Space

Imagine yourself selected to be the first kid to ever travel into space! Out of all the schoolchildren in America, you have been chosen to go to the Kennedy Space Center and ride with the astronauts to the International Space Station. Once there, you'll conduct experiments and be a working member of the Discovery crew. Are you up to it? Good. Let's go.

Your first stop will be the space camp in Florida (*http://spacecamp.com*). There are three of these space camps now, and kids can learn a lot about what will happen at the Kennedy Space Center by attending one of these camps. Your second stop will be at the spaceport itself, and you will be given a virtual tour of the place on arrival (*http://www.kennedyspacecenter.com*).

Before things get too serious, NASA will send you to two places for training. The first is *http://www.kidsnspace.org* and the second will be *http://starchild.gsfc. nasa.gov/ docs/StarChild/StarChild.html*. During these visits you'll select your experiments and learn about the Hubble telescope.

The pictures that have been taken by this huge telescope have broadened man's knowledge of outer space a great deal. The Hubble is massive in size, as you will see *(http://starchild.gsfc.nasa.gov/docs/starchild/space_level2_kennedy.html)*.

There are two sets of photos that you can study before leaving earth, but neither will prepare you for what you will actually see out there. The first set is actual pictures taken by the Hubble in its first year. Take a look at this picture: *http://oposite.stsci.edu/pubinfo/pictures.html*. The second set of pictures is from the official NASA photojournal, and you will be given a set of these photos when you return to Earth *(http://www.as.wvu.edu/~planet)*.

You will, of course, be riding the space shuttle today. You've probably seen it take off and land on television many times *(http://www.j-2.com/space/landing.htm)*.

We can't pay a kid to serve aboard a spacecraft, but when you return the Mission Commander will let you have anything you want from the space shop at the Kennedy Space Center *(http://www.spaceshop.com)*. Why don't you browse around and select something for your family when you get back?

Okay, space kid, time to suit up. All of the kids in America will be rooting for you today as you blast off!

This is how a simple Inquiry and Exploration journey is developed. Since no formal learning is required under this design, the student simply browses the presecured sites, collects information, and becomes increasingly excited about the forthcoming space unit.

You, the teacher, have written a script and expanded it with highly visual supplements that are both contextual and relevant for the intended learning. While we can't show you them in this book as colorful highlights, these sites would be direct connections or links as soon as the lesson is placed on the Internet.

Teachers could send these lessons via e-mail to students (and parents) as homework, or simply make them available as an item on a web page to be selected on the main screen. The procedure is both safe and informative. Now, let's look at some sample journeys in each of the eight designs.

JOURNEYS: USING THE EIGHT DESIGNS

In Chapter 3 we introduced eight types of curriculum:

Content-based

Skill-based

Inquiry and Exploration

Conceptual learning

Interdisciplinary

Title of Activity:_____Time Required:_____
Grade Level(s): _____   Lesson Designer(s):_____

Curriculum Design (check off below):
☐ Content-Based
☐ Skill-Based
☐ Inquiry & Exploration
☐ Conceptual
☐ Interdisciplinary
☐ Cooperative
☐ Problem-Solving
☐ Critical & Creative Thinking

Online Resources/References:

Sunshine State Standards (Outcomes):

Materials Needed:

Figure 4.1 Internet Lesson Planning Template

1. Introduction. General description in narrative form. It could contain an overview of the process/tasks, expected outcomes, evaluation criteria, and roles of participants—for example, "You are an astronaut exploring our solar system."

2. Questioning and Planning. (Could be eliminated for more linear curriculum design models.) Students should create their own questions to help guide their inquiry.

- What do we know?
- What do we need to know?
- Who is going to do what?
- What resources/materials do we need to complete the tasks?

3. Process/Tasks. (Depends on curriculum design, but uses online references/resources on front side.)

Outcome & Evaluation
- Outcome could simply be heightened interest, acquired skills, or a tangible product such as a project, presentation, or paper.
- Evaluation method: Explain how students will be graded. Will a rubric be developed?

Cooperative learning

Problem-solving

Critical and creative thinking

The evolution of these curricula from Content-Based through Critical and Creative Thinking is centered around greater involvement of the student and greater application of the learning. We will examine these eight designs through sample curriculum journeys using the Internet. All the examples are built using the Planning template in this chapter and contain the following basic elements.

Lesson Format

1. Lesson title
2. Type of curriculum design
3. Appropriate grade levels
4. Type of activity
5. Journey references (websites) (topics found in Resource E)
6. Student outcomes
7. The curriculum journey

Teachers in schools who begin to create Internet-assisted lessons will want to share these lessons with other teachers in their schools and across the world. A simple but standard format will increase communication about such lessons.

CONTENT-BASED LESSONS

Content-based lessons are by far the most common curriculum design found in schools. The design identifies in advance those ideas to be learned or mastered by the student; these are usually organized as a discipline of study or subject. The curriculum itself consists of critical data or knowledge that represents what currently is known about the subject area.

 ## Journey — All The World Is A Stage

Grade Level: 10th to 12th

Activity Type: Data gathering in specific content areas

Search Topics/Keywords: British Literature, Drama, Museums, World Literature

Outcome: Students will acquire knowledge about British literature and theater.

Today you are going to England. First you will tour some sites in London and its surrounding boroughs. While in London you will stop at the newly constructed Globe Theatre and learn about it. You will then venture to other sites related to the Globe, William Shakespeare, and Hamlet. This journey will take about 90 minutes.

The first stop is *http://www.southwark.gov.uk/tourism*. Click on "Places to Visit" and/or the "Tour" button. Scroll down to the Globe Theatre and click. Complete the following:

1. Name the London borough in which the original Globe Theater was located.

   _____

2. In addition to the Globe, name three other theaters.

   a. _____

   b. _____

   c. _____

3. When was the first Globe Theatre built at Shoreditch?

   _____

4. The first Globe Theatre was moved and then burned to the ground in what year?

5. How many persons can the new Globe Theatre hold, both sitting and standing?

6. Find three additional interesting facts about the Globe Theatre or Elizabethan theater going from this site.

   a. _____

   b. _____

   c. _____

7. Using this same site, choose another famous place such as the George Inn or the Dungeon and for this place, list three known facts.

   a. _____

   b. _____

   c. _____

Your second stop is *http://www.rdg.ac.uk/Globe*. Find the following by clicking on "Shakespeare's Globe" (in the middle of the screen).

8. In what year did the Puritans finally close the Globe Theatre? _____

Now, on the left scroll bar, scroll down to "Virtual Reality Views" of the rebuilt Globe and click. Then click on the "Virtual Tour" of the Globe Theatre but *do not* click on the virtual reality views of the unfinished theater. Navigate around the views and the text and gather the following data.

9. How much was admission to view the play from the following sections of the theater?

   a. Groundlings (the yard) _____

   b. Lower gallery _____

   c. Gentlemen's room _____

10. Based on this information, name two advantages of sitting in the gentlemen's section:

   a. _____

   b. _____

11. What was the favored sitting area of the aristocrats? (Hint: it was not one of the three above areas.)

   a. _____

   b. _____

   c. _____

12. Why do you think they favored this area?

   _____

13. What is pictured on the "Frons Scenaie" (the stage wall/backdrop)?

   _____

14. View the yard section and list two facts you found interesting.

   _____

Your third and fourth stops are *http://members.tripod.com/flood5549/globe.html* and *http://www.calvin.edu/academic/engl/346/proj/nathan/globe.htm.*

15. From the above two sites find five additional facts about the Globe Theatre not already listed as an answer:

   a. _____

   b. _____

   c. _____

   d. _____

   e. _____

Choose your own fifth stop. Using the search engine of your choice (Yahoo, Magellan, or another), search for an informative site about William Shakespeare.

16. For this site, list its address _____

   and add five facts you have learned about William Shakespeare.

   a. _____

   b. _____

   c. _____

   d. _____

   e. _____

Your sixth stop is *http://members.tripod.com/~Moon.Faerv/hamlet.html.* Find the following.

17. What college was Hamlet attending?

_____

18. Who did the senior Hamlet kill the day Hamlet was born (Act 1)?

_____

19. In what country is Hamlet set?

_____

20. What is the name of the castle in Hamlet?

_____

21. Identify two themes in Hamlet:
     a. _____
     b. _____

Choose your own seventh stop. Find some informative sites on Hamlet.

22. List the web address of a particularly good Hamlet site.
    http://_____

23. From the site you identified in Question 22, list five facts about Hamlet not previously identified:
     a. _____
     b. _____
     c. _____
     d. _____
     e. _____

Now, for the truly adventurous web travelers:

Bonus #1. What is the name of the real castle in Denmark that Hamlet's castle represents? _____

The source of this information is the following website:
http://_____

Bonus #2. Who built this castle between 1574 and 1585? _____

The source of this information is the following website:
http://_____

Author's note: While the teacher is covering facts in a direct manner, the student is being allowed to explore the net without direct supervision on some of the questions. What happens to the curriculum when each student has the freedom to select his or her own sites?

JOURNEY — THE MAYFLOWER

Grade Level: 1st to 3rd

Activity Type: Knowledge acquisition

Search Topics/Keywords: Colonial America

Outcome: Students will know the story of the *Mayflower,* a historical American point of reference.

The Pilgrims came to our country on ships such as the *Mayflower.* Today, we will be visiting some Internet sites as a group (using a TV monitor) to learn some things about the Pilgrims' voyage on the *Mayflower.*

Let's study the ship. What materials were used to build it *(http://nanosft.com/ plymouth/mayflower.html)?*

Here we see a picture of the *Mayflower.* It was a pretty small ship made of tree trunks, mud, and tar. Nails were used in some of the planks, but mostly the boards were fitted together. The sails were heavy linens, like sheets.

Who were the passengers? Were most of the passengers men or women *(http:// teacher.scholastic.com/thanksgiving/mayflower/tour/index.htm)?*

Here is a list of the 102 passengers and 30 crew members who sailed on the voyage to America: *http://members.aol.com/calebj/passenger.html.* Some of the passengers were women and children. Life was very hard for them and they had many chores each day.

What did the Mayflower smell like? Did the passengers have cabins on the ship? Could children take their pets along? How did people go to the bathroom on such a crowded ship? What happened when a big storm came along? *http://teacher.scholastic. com/thanksgiving/interviews/ask_kate_mayflower.htm*

List five interesting things you learned about the the Mayflower today:
1. _____
2. _____
3. _____
4. _____
5. _____

What are two things you'd still like to know about the Mayflower?
1. _____
2. _____

Use the lesson websites to look for the answers.

Author's note: Students, especially young students, need background knowledge for further learning. Almost everything we learn is defined in terms of what we already know (associative learning). Selecting the best foundational knowledge (representative learning) is an important part of instructional planning.

SKILL-BASED LESSONS

Many states have adopted competency-based testing that causes the curriculum to focus squarely on skills acquisition in the classroom. There are two common types of skill lessons in schools; acquiring basic skills such as reading, writing, and computation; and understanding and applying a basic process. In both cases, an operation is repeated until competence is achieved (practice effect). Both types of skill-based instruction can be aided by resources found on the Internet.

 Journey — Math Skills Review & Practice (Three Stations)

Grade Level: 3rd to 5th

Activity Type: Skills acquisition and practice

Search Topics/Keywords: Addition, Division, Math History, Measurement, Baseball

Outcome: Practice and review in basic math computation.

    a. Student will demonstrate mastery of basic facts.

    b. Student will apply math skills in problem-solving activities.

Mastery of the "operations" in math is a prerequisite to higher-level activity. Today, such mastery should reflect national standards established by the National Council of Teachers of Mathematics as well as respective state standards of achievement. Two good Internet sources for determining state standards are *http://www.pbs.org/ teacher source* and *http://www.explorasource.com.*

There are many sources on the Internet to reinforce skill mastery. Early references for lesson planning include ERIC lesson plans, *(http://askeric.org/virtual/lessons)* and the Gateway to Educational Materials at *http://www.thegateway.org.* In addition, worksheets for practice can be "pulled down" at any level and in any subject at *http://www.sssoftware.com/freeworksheets.*

Today's review is to determine if you can use the basic operations (addition, subtraction, multiplication, and division), understand fractions, and graph the results of problems. Your first level of mastery demonstration is to complete exercises using flashcards (addition, subtraction, multiplication, division) at *http://www.aplusmath.com.* When you can demonstrate 80% mastery on drill exercises, the teacher will verify your passage to Station 2, math applications.

Station 2 math problems focus on 5 of 11 areas at *http://www.pbs,org/ teachersource/math/elementary_analysis.shtm.*

Complete the following activities:

    Activity 1: Neighborhood Math (The Mall)

    Activity 2: Counting Calories

    Activity 3: Weather/Rainfall Graphing

Activity 1: The Car Wash/Spreadsheets

Activity 1: Weather/Temperature Measurement

Extra-Credit Activity: Calculate Leaping Lemurs of Madagascar at *http://www. pbs.org/edens/madagascar.*

When you have completed these skill application problems, the teacher will verify your passage to Station 3, math problem-solving.

You may select any one of the problems listed at *http://www.funbrain.com.* In addition, if your math profile is weak in division, complete the baseball activity at this site as well.

Author's note: Basic skills are those everyday operations that we conduct at home, at the store, and at work. Useful applications are plentiful (for example, figuring baseball batting averages is the way many boys learn division. Why do schools use drill in isolation so often in teaching basic skills?

 Journey — Quadratic Equations

Grade Level: 8th to 12th

Activity Type: Understanding and applying a process

Search Topics/Keywords: Algebra, Quadratic Equations, Satellites, Sputnik

Outcomes:
  a. Student understands the purpose of a quadratic equation.
  b. Student can solve problems using quadratic equations.
  c. Student can apply quadratic equations in space program scenarios.

Students learn in the primary grades that numerals represent real objects. They also learn that such objects/numerals can be manipulated through basic operations such as addition and subtraction and that this can be done with incomplete and partial objects (decimals, fractions) as well.

When students enter the next level of abstraction (algebra, geometry, trigonometry, and calculus), they are no longer manipulating real objects, instead they're using formulae to solve problems containing unknowns.

Using these formulae and procedures (proofs), mathematical relationships on earth and in space can be verified. Algebra is the first instance where formulae are shown to be reliable in solving problems involving unknowns. Reference *http://www.ms.uky.edu/~carl/ma330/project2/al-khwa21.html* and/or *http://www.museums. reading.ac.uk/vmoc/algebra.*

Quadratic equations are formulae for understanding nonlinear or irregular mathematical relationships. They are used to solve puzzles and unknowns. Reference *http://www.unican.es/sosmath/algebra/quadraticeq/bdef/bdef.html.*

What is meant by the statement at the above site that quadratic equations are "puzzles that are glued together"?

_____

_____

_____

Solving problems using quadratic equations is a process of finding relationships among unknowns. Reference _http://members.tripod.com/~kselva/quad.html_ and _http://www.webmath.com/quad.html_. Using the 13-step process provided at _http://www.quickmath.com_, solve a quadratic equation. When you've completed the equation, take the practice test at _http://math.rice.edu/~lanius/Lessons_.

If you need further assistance, reference _http://math.rice.edu_.

Finally, what problems relating to orbits of satellites such as Sputnik (_http://sputnik.infospace.ru_) might be solved by using quadratic equations? Is there a useful formula?

Author's note: In these examples of skills development, the student is directed to sites where traditional practice can occur. Once mastery is achieved, the student is asked to apply these skills to real-world problems. Could we create "chains" of basic skills leading from mastery to application in the real world?

INQUIRY AND EXPLORATION LESSONS

As in our construction example, First Kid in Space, inquiry lessons seek to satisfy natural curiosity by students or to introduce topic areas without mastery requirements. This type of lesson is often used to motivate students to learn about an unknown subject area. In the example below, the teacher is beginning a world geography unit and wants students to explore some countries of the world. The teacher puts herself into the lesson to catch the students' attention.

 Journey — The Adventures of Miss Shell

Grade Level: 4th to 8th

Activity Type: Acquisition of background information

Search Topics/Keywords: Paris, Africa, South Africa, Kruger Park, Italy, Sri Lanka, Madagascar, and India.

Outcomes:
  a. Students will gain knowledge of three countries other than their own.
  b. Student will develop an interest in places other than where they live.
  c. Students will apply skills in planning a trip.

Miss Shell is a wonderful teacher who loves to travel to exotic places. But how is she to do this when she teaches every day in the fifth grade? Her secret is that on Monday, Wednesday, and Friday she slips away for twenty minutes and goes to her computer and . . . well, you know.

Monday. If this is Monday, mused Miss Shell, this must be Paris! Paris, France, the "City of Lights." The very name has a magic ring to it; Paris is a place of beauty, art, and romance. Located in Europe, surrounded by Spain, Belgium, Germany, Switzerland, Austria, and Luxembourg, France is the heart of the continent, and Paris, the very heart of France.

You can get to Paris from the United States by many modes of transportation. Miss Shell could book a direct flight *(http:www.directflightsavers.com)* or she could take a slow freighter *(http://www.freighterworld.com)*.

Which do you recommend?   _____

Which is less expensive ?   _____

Anyway, it's a short lunch period so Miss Shell flies to Orly Airport and consults her subway guide for the ride into the city *(http://www.paris.org/Metro)*. Miss Shell is annoyed because it is raining. She could have prepared for this by checking *http://www.intellicast.com/LocalWeather/World/content.shtml*.

What is the weather like today in Paris? _____

Miss Shell wants to stay near the Notre Dame cathedral so she selects the Hotel des Grand Ecoles *(www.hotel-grandes-ecoles.com)*.

Can you describe the courtyard?   _____

Getting a little hungry, Miss Shell stops at a great French restaurant near the Pont Neuf called The Coté Seine *(http://www.coteseine.fr/carte.htm)*.

Can you recommend something from the menu? Remember, one dollar is equal to seven francs.(Be careful! Teachers aren't rich, you know.)

_____

_____

Consulting her travel guide, Miss Shell plans her day carefully. She must see the Eiffel Tower, a city icon *(http://www.paris.org/Monuments)*, and the Notre Dame cathedral *(http://paris-tourism.com)*, and probably the Louvre *(http://www.louvre.fr)*, a world-famous art gallery.

Can you name the most famous painting in this museum? _____

_____

If time permits, Miss Shell would also like to see the National Art Center *(http://infoeagle.bc.edu/bc_org/avp/cas/fnart/arch/pompidou.html)* and perhaps the Museum de Orsay *(http://www.smartweb.fr/fr/orsay)*.

"Darn it," said Miss Shell. It was time to go back to class and she hadn't even been to the Moulin Rouge.

Do you know what that is? *(http://www.francetourism.com)*?_____

_____

_____

Wednesday. Today, I'm going on Safari, thought Miss Shell. She had always wanted to go to Africa (http://www.inform.umd.edu/mdk-12/homepers/africa). Did you know that Africa is twice as big as the continental United States?

There are forty nations in Africa, and each one has a unique culture (http://www.africana.com). Miss Shell did a little reading about the individual countries so that she could select one (http://www.jao.com/africa/index.html).

Miss Shell didn't want to see Africa from some tour bus. She wanted to get out among the people and see all the sights. She found a man with a 1974 Volkswagen Beetle who was going to drive through Africa. Want to come along (http://www.stoessel.ch/beetle_africa.htm)?

By the way, what happened to the car on the trip?

If you are going to Africa, you must go on safari, and Miss Shell found a great game park in eastern South Africa (http://www.ecoafrica.com/krugerpark/sighting.htm). What did people see today at Kruger?

Do you know what five animals are considered to be the most important to see on a real safari? Look for the answer at http://www.africaphotosafaris.co.za.

Miss Shell was admiring the picture she took of an elephant (http://www.nature.wildlife.com/ele.82html) when the bell rang. "Time to get back to the children," she murmured as she shut down her computer.

Friday. Because it's Friday, Miss Shell wants to go somewhere really exotic, and she selects Sri Lanka.

Most people don't even know where Sri Lanka is or that it used to be called Ceylon. If you'll look near the tip of India, you'll see it.

The reason Miss Shell wants to go to this island nation is because of its biodiversity. Most island nations have unique wildlife and plants, and Sri Lanka is a special place in this respect (http://despardes.com/travel.html). To know more about the country you can look at http://www.yahooligans.com/Around_the_World/Countries/Sri_Lanka/Maps.

In particular, Miss Shell is here to see the butterflies of Sri Lanka (http://www.wht.org). Miss Shell uses all her film taking pictures of the insects and the countryside. Would you like to see the photos? Go to http://www.math.bgsu.edu/~mabhaya/photo/photo_album.html.

Wow, thought Miss Shell, this was an exciting week! Next week, thought Miss Shell, I'd really like to visit India and Peru and . . . .

Author's note: This sort of exploratory journey can be developed by the student. Making the student the subject of the activity increases student motivation. This type of journey can be linked to a more detailed study of a topic, the application of skills, or a new interdisciplinary understanding of the world. What happens to student motivation when the lesson is about the student?

Journey — Beneath the Seas

Grade Level: 5th to 8th

Activity Type: Conceptual orientation

Search Topics/Keywords: Oceans, Cousteau, Treasure Hunts, Underseas
   Environment, Submarines, Sharks

Outcome: Students will be able to construct a conceptual map of the oceans, an
   area covering the vast majority of the earth's surface.

The United States is bounded by two oceans, the Atlantic on the east and the Pacific
on the west. In addition, the Gulf of Mexico lies along about two-thirds of our southern boundary. It makes sense, then, that oceans will play an important role in our future, and we need to be knowledgeable about them. Today you will become an
oceanographer, a person who studies the oceans.

   The following Internet sites will introduce you to ocean studies: *http://www.
ocean.98.org* and *http://www.scrtec.org/track/tracks/f011600.html.*

   We all possess some knowledge about oceans, even if just from watching the movie
Jaws. Sharks have always fascinated man; they are one symbol of the mysteries of
the ocean. If you want to know more about "sharks down there," check out *http://
www.ozemail.com.au/~bilsons/SHARKS.htm*   or   *http://www.nationalgeographic.com/
features/97/sharks.*

   The person who has done the most to help us learn about the oceans of the
world is Jacques Cousteau, a Frenchman who for years sailed the oceans and explored beneath the seas. To learn more about this man and his legacy, visit
http://www.incwell.com/Biographies/Cousteau.html   and   *http://www.egroups.com/group/
acquanet.*

   Another way to learn about the oceans is through the active treasure hunting that
is ongoing in many areas. During the Age of Exploration of the Americas (1500–1800)
the Spanish, Dutch, British, and French competed for the mineral wealth found in the
New World. As they shipped these fortunes back to Europe, many of the ships were
sunk by storms. Today, particularly off the coast of Florida, active treasure hunting
continues. If you want to know more about these treasure hunts, visit *http://mem-
bers.tripod.com, http://www.melfisher.com,* or *http://www.onlinether.com.*

   Scientists have actually learned a lot more about the oceans than most people re-
alize. Studies of the ocean floor *(http://www-odp.tamu.edu),* the currents under the
seas *(http://www.tamu.edu/woce/Introduction.html),* and the coral reefs *(http://state-of-
coast.nosa.gov)* are extensive. There are also many environmental concerns
(http://www.seasky.org/sea6.html or *http://www.bsac.com/world/nature/naturenews.htm)*
related to oceans.

   Currently, man relies heavily on submarines to conduct studies under the seas. If
you want to know more about these vehicles, visit these three sites: *http://www.geocities
.com/pentagon/Quarters/7433, http://ussubs.com/lead.html,* and *http://www.caribsub.com.*

Eventually, man will live under the seas because of the need for space or to be closer to many natural resources, including food sources. If you'd like to know more about such efforts, see *http://www.enteractive.com/jmcousteau/pages/tour1.htm*. If you'd like a good source for books and photographs about the oceans of the world, visit *http://www.oceangallery.com*.

Assignment:

Now that you have visited these sites and learned a little about the world beneath the seas, begin constructing a road map for future exploration of the oceans by creating a list of at least 20 items related to the oceans that should be learned or explored during your lifetime.

Author's note: Having each student submit a list of topics could lead to a master list of interests and then to a plan for a unit to study the oceans of the world. Using this technique, each student could study an area of personal interest. Is it necessary that all students study the same materials?

CONCEPTUAL LEARNING

Curriculum designs that feature a conceptual focus seek to promote student understanding of general ideas, not detailed information. Sometimes, however, a concept can emerge from the study of specific information. In this example, "Flight", the student is given specific information about flight theory and is led to an understanding of man's ability to fly.

 Journey — Flight

Grade Level: 5th to 7th

Activity Type: Conceptual construction

Search Topics/Keywords: Inventions, Machines, Science, Museums, Experiments

Outcomes:

   a. Student will master specific factual information about flying.
   b. Student will apply skills of inquiry.
   c. Student will conceptualize the act of flying using machines.

You will be working with a partner to become an expert aerospace engineer and aircraft pilot.

1. Draw a simple Venn diagram to compare aeronautical engineering to aerospace engineering (*http://wings.ucdavis.edu/Book/Flight/intermediate/aeronautics-01.html*).

2. Describe the difference between aerodynamics and gas dynamics. (*http://wings. ucdavis.edu/Book/Flight/intermediate/gas-01.html*).

_____

_____

3. What five units of measurement are useful for the study of flight? Give an example of each one (*http://wings.ucdavis.edu/Books/Flight/intermediate/move-01.html*).

_____

_____

_____

_____

_____

4. What is Mach 1 and how fast is it (*http://wings.ucdavis.edu/Book/Flight/intermediate/move-01.html*)?

_____

_____

5. Now it's time for a little flight training. Go to: *http://www.planemath.com/ activities/pmenterprises/index.html.*
   Enter the Training Department and choose "Forces of Flight" to complete the following:
   a. Describe the four forces which allow a plane to fly.

_____

_____

_____

_____

   b. Explain Bernoulli's principle in words or pictures.

   c. Sketch an aerodynamic plane.

_____

   d. Why does a crumpled piece of paper fall to the floor more quickly than a flat piece of paper?

_____

_____

e. Which of the following conditions will increase the speed of a plane?

   a. thrust < drag

   b. thrust = drag

   c. thrust > drag

Now, choose the "Tour of the Basics" and complete the following:

f. How does a propeller provide thrust?

_____

_____

g. What part of a plane's wing allows it to bank?

_____

_____

h. Explain why a pilot lowers the wing flaps when landing.

_____

_____

i. What allows the plane to "yaw"?

_____

_____

j. What controls the "pitch" of the plane?

_____

_____

k. Use your hand to demonstrate "pitch" and "yaw" to your partner.

And they said it couldn't be done! Visit the Virtual Flight Museum site at *http://hawaii/psychology.msstate.edu/invent* and complete the following activities by reading an article from the 1905 *Scientific American.*

1. Explain how the author feels about the Wright brothers' first flight.

_____

_____

2. Determine how much farther and longer (distance and time) the Wright brothers' flight of September 29th was than the September 26th flight. (Hint: choose "Just Off the Runway.")

_____

_____

3. Describe Clement Adler's role in the development of the airplane. (Hint: choose "Inventors Gallery.")

_____

_____

4. Fly the 1903 Wright Flyer simulator.

And now for some PlaneMath! Visit the site *http://www.planemath-com/activities/pmactivitiesall.html* and choose "Applying Flying." With your partner, complete these activities.

1. Flight Path
2. Plane Capacity
3. Fill 'er Up
4. Lift-Off.

Try flying on your own. Design, build, and fly your own plane with your partner. Be sure to try modifications to improve your plane's flight speed and distance. Record the data and graph your flight data or create a spreadsheet. You've earned your wings ! Check out these sites.

http://www.skyharbour.com

http://www.sprocketworks.com

http://www.al.com/children/flyact.htm

For more high-flying fun, check out:

http://www.nasa.gov/kids/html

http://www.af.mil.aflinkjr

http://wings.ucdavis.edu/index.html

http://www.planemath.com

Author's note: Conceptual learning can be conducted at many levels of abstraction. Generally, with younger students who lack life experiences, more foundational knowledge must be provided in order to gain basic understanding. How would concept designs be different for students in 3rd, 8th, and 11th grades?

 Journey — Planets out There

Grade Level: 3rd to 5th

Activity Type: conceptual orientation

Search Topics/Keywords: Planets, Mars, Asteroids, Hubble

Outcomes:

a. Students will develop a conceptual map of outer space.
b. Students will use information gained to determine areas of interest for continued study.

Today you are going to learn about outer space and the bodies in our universe. Scientists who study the stars and planets are called astronomers, and today your task is to gather information about objects in space and decide what you'd like to learn more about as an astronomer.

Astronomers have long studied the planets and stars. Our knowledge of both has greatly increased in the last 20 years, largely due to improvements in technology. Much of our recent knowledge has come from the Hubble telescope (*http://opisite. stsci.edu/pubinfo/pictures.html*). Check out the pictures!

In order to begin thinking about outer space, start with a virtual space tour (*http://library.thinkquest.org/25401/data/tour/index.html*). You may also want to view some planetary simulations at *http://space.jpl.nasa.gov.*

One planet that has always fascinated man is Mars. Known as the "red" planet, Mars has been the source of much science fiction. It was thought for years that Mars was the planet most likely to support life similar to ours. Visit these Mars sites: *http://www.mpfwww.pjl.nasa.gov/med/science/index.html, http://cmex.arc.nasa.gov, http:// www.scifan.com/science/mars,* and *http://www.solar-system.co.uk.*

There is a great deal of interest in asteroids, mainly due to television and movies. Can these large celestial bodies really threaten earth? See *http:// impact.arc.nasa. gov/index.html* to find out about possible hazards. Other interesting asteroid sites include *http://www.bloomington.in.us/~jashoup/space/astro.htm* and *http://www.as.wvu. edu/~planet/ink_solr.htm* where you can view pictures of asteroids. For facts about asteroids, see *http://www.worldbook.com/fun/bth/meteorites/ html/meteorites.html.*

Armed with this new knowledge about outer space, the planets, and asteroids, write a short story about space exploration in the year 2010. Be sure and use some of the facts you have learned about planets, asteroids, and stars in your story. At the conclusion of your story, list three questions you would like answered in our upcoming unit on space.

Author's note: Unlike the Flight example, this conceptual activity asks the student to arrange the information found at sites into a meaningful whole using a short story. As the student orders the facts, certain questions will become the organizers and motivators for further inquiry and study. How does student-centered learning differ from the more traditional teacher-controlled learning?

INTERDISCIPLINARY DESIGNS

When teachers desire that students make a connection among subjects or between a single subject and the real world, they employ an interdisciplinary design. In the United States, middle schools use these designs to give the students general understanding prior to secondary study. Interdisciplinary learning can feature various levels of sophistication, even within the same classroom, and can provide opportunities for the application of this knowledge in the real world.

Journey — Cultures of the World

Grade Level: 5th to 8th

Activity Type: Compare and contrast

Search Topics/Keywords: Cultures, Religions, Languages, Flags, Wedding Customs, India, Madagascar, New Zealand.

Outcomes:
   a. Student will become familiar with three different cultures.
   b. Student will compare and contrast these cultures according to symbols, history, language, and religions.
   c. Student will define culture in everyday operational terms.

Culture is a difficult thing to understand. When we are confronted with a language, religion, or custom different from our own, we often wonder why other people aren't like us. In this lesson, you will be asked to learn about several cultures that are different from that of the United States. You will try to determine just what a culture is, and you will become more aware of your own culture through a process of comparison and contrast. You may even gain a better understanding of the place from which your ancestors came.

First, let's find out what the dictionary says about the word *culture*. Write the definition of culture, using this site: *http://work.ucsd.edu:5141/cgi-bin/http_webster.*

_____

_____

Let's study some exotic cultures that aren't like ours. How about India, New Zealand, and Madagascar? Great sources for finding out about these countries are the *CIA Fact Book (http://www.odci.gov/cia/publications//pubs.html)* and the Web Virtual Library, found at *http://vlib.stanford.edu/Overview2.html.*

You may need to brush up on your map skills if you can't mentally locate these places. Two general sites to use are *http://www.maps.co.nz* for New Zealand and *http://www.mapsofindia.com/link.html* for India. To find Madagascar, check out *http://www.nationalgeographic.com/maps.*

Now that you know the location of these countries, can you make a guess about the weather in these places? (Hint: consider latitude.) Do you think weather in the United States affects how people in various regions live?

Yes_____

No_____

What languages do you think are spoken in these localities? Would you like to learn a few words of a different language? Check out phrases in 66 different languages at *http://www.travellang.com/languages* or, if you wish, translate something you want to say at *http://www.logos.it.* Some languages you can learn in high school are

French (*http://www.ambafrance.org/ALF*), German (*http://www.snowcrest.net*), Spanish (*http://www.studyspanish.com*) or even romantic Italian (*http://www.cyberitalian.com*).

How do you think these languages influence culture?

_____

The flags of each nation are interesting because they tend to display symbols of each culture. Many Muslim nations, for instance, have swords on their flags. Take a look at *http://www.theodora.com/flags.html* and find several flags of countries in the Middle East.

The United States flag has thirteen red and white stripes representing our first colonies. Look at the flags of Egypt, Japan, and Brazil.

Can you make any statement about the flags and the culture of a country?

_____

_____

_____

Religions, too, are an important part of any culture since they formalize the beliefs of the people in that society.

Can you guess what religions you would find in New Zealand, Madagascar, or India?

_____

On what did you base your observation or guess?

_____

Holidays often tell us a lot about a culture. In the United States, for instance, we celebrate the Fourth of July. Do you know why? France celebrates a similar holiday on the 14th of July—Bastille Day. What holidays do you suppose they celebrate in New Zealand (*http://www.nzway.co.nz/*) in India (*http://www.geocities.com/collegepark/lounge/5662*), or in Madagascar (*http://www.madagascar-guide.com/top/HP_FriEng.html*)?

Which holiday would you like to attend?

_____

History also plays a major role in determining the culture of a country or region. Read briefly about the history of India (*http://itihass.com*), Madagascar (*http://iias.leiduniv.nl/iiasn/iiasn7/ellis.html*) and New Zealand (*http://discovernz.co.nz*).List below some of the historical events in each country that you believe influence the way the people think and what they value.

India

_____

Madagascar

_____

New Zealand

_____

It is interesting that different cultures often value the same things even though their histories, religions, and languages vary. For example, both New Zealand and Madagascar highly value wildlife; since both are island nations, they have a wide variety of plants and animals (*http://parks.yahoo.com* and *http://www.infoamp.net/~ornst/madagascar.html*). The protection of rare birds, fish, and plants is a national value.

Finally, we can look at one custom, weddings, to see how much diversity there is in the world and how it is acceptable to celebrate the same kind of occasion in different ways. Check out the customs in these places:

Africa—*http://melanet.com/awg*

Scotland—*http://weddingcircle.com/ethnic/scot*

Japan—*http://www.Japan.guide.com/e/e2061.html*

Israel—*http://weddingcircle.com/ethnic/jewish*

Now you have examined history, languages, religions, holidays, climates, and a common celebration ceremony.

In your own words, what is a culture?

_____

_____

Before we leave this lesson, let's apply what we have discovered to our own culture. Remember, we learned that our flag represents our new colonies (and the stars represent each present state).

What other historical events do we acknowledge with a symbol (money) or a holiday?

_____

_____

What are the major languages spoken in the United States?

_____

_____

Do we have a national religion? Do you know why or why not?

_____

Do we celebrate religious holidays? Can you name several?

_____

Are there questions you'd like to ask your teacher about our culture or other cultures in the world?

_____

Author's note: The design of an interdisciplinary curriculum allows expansion into subject matter, social issues, and even interpersonal applications. The flexibility of interdisciplinary units allows understanding to occur at many levels of complexity and through many mediums. How could the interdisciplinary unit be used to accomodate a wide range of learners in the classroom?

COOPERATIVE LEARNING DESIGNS

Over the past decade, many schools have tried to implement cooperative learning as an instructional strategy. CL is also a curriculum design because it causes learning to be focused on the interaction among students in the learning process. Beyond achievement, byproducts of this process are vital work skills for the 21st century, including planning, sharing, and accepting others.

Cooperative learning has many configurations, such as "jigsaw," Teams-Games-Tournaments (TGT), and various student teams and cross-age models. Each of these subdesigns affects how students are treated and how students learn in the classroom setting.

 Journey — What is Pollution?

Grade Levels: 5th to 9th

Activity Type: Cooperative/share pair/jigsaw model

Search Topics/Keywords: Acid Rain, Air Pollution, Wetlands , Environment, Global Warming, Noise Pollution, Rain Forests, Water Pollution, Waste Management

Outcomes: Using cooperative learning techniques (the jigsaw), each student will

    a. Conduct primary study of one form of pollution.
    b. Present to other group members his or her findings.
    c. Collectively define what is and is not pollution.
    d. Identify common examples of pollution in the community.

A primary study group of six students will be assigned to study the topic of pollution and apply its finding via an analysis sheet. Three types of pollution will be assessed: air pollution, water pollution, and noise pollution. Two students (share/pair) will be assigned to each type of pollution. Within each group, individual students will have an assigned specialty, such as the greenhouse effect, wetlands, global warming, rain forests, or waste management.

Listed below are the sites students are to visit while completing the analysis sheet.

Topic 1: Air Pollution

    Student 1: Acid Rain

    Student 2: Global Warming

Air Pollution—General

Glossary of Terms
http://www.shsu.edu/~chemistry/glossary/glos.html

Update from the EPA
http://www.epa.gov/airnow

Polluting Industries
http://www.pirg.org/envion/energy/lethal98/index.htm

World with No Cars
http://radawana.cg.tuwian.ac.at/~martinpi/nocar.html

Acid Rain (Student 1, Group 1)

ABC's of Acid Rain
http://qlink.queensu.ca/~4lrm4/table.htm

Frequent Questions
http://www.ns.ec.gc.ca/aeb/ssd/acid/acidfaq.html

Laws and Regulations
http://www.epa.gov//acidrain/ardhome.html

Global Warming (Student 2, Group 1)

Warming Update
http://wwwlaw.pace.edu/env/energy/globalwarming.html

Greenhouse Network
http://www.greenhousenet.org

The Future
http://www.envionweb.org/edf

Topic 2: Water Pollution

Student 1: rain forests

Student 2: wetlands

Water Pollution

About Water Pollution
http://www.nce.unr.edu/swp/default.asp

Don't Flush This
http://wsa.co.uk

MBTEs in Drinking Water
http://epa.gov/safewater/mbte.html

Rain Forest (Student 1, Group 2)

Rain Forest Workshop
http://kids.oed.wednet.edu/marshall/homepage/tropical.html

Statistics and Photos
http://www.rainforests.net

Ecology Sites
http://geocities.yahoo.com/cgi-bio/hood/geo?hood-rainforest

Wetlands (Student 2, Group 2)

Wetlands—EPA Site
http://www.epa.gov.OWOW/wetlands/vital/toc.html

The Estuary
http://www.estuarylive.org

Contaminants
http://www.time.com/time/reports/environment/heroes/contaminants

Topic 3: Noise Pollution

Student 1: sounds

Student 2: controls

Noise Pollution

Effects of Noise
http://www.nonoise.org/library/suter/suter.htm.

Antinoise Information
http://www.lhh.org/noise/index.htm

Sounds (Student 1, Group 3)

Music and Noise
http://www.lhh.org/noise/facts/music.htm

Sounds of a Rain Forest
http://www.naturenet.com.br

Controls (Student 2, Group 3)

Laws to Control Noise
http://www.internetnorth.com

All six students in the Cooperative Learning group will respond to the following questions while reading in their subareas:

1. What is meant by pollution ?

2. Give an example from what you have read of a kind of pollution about which you know.

3. Is this kind of pollution found where you live?

After each of the six students has read his or her section, taken notes, and answered these three questions, students will meet to teach each other what they have learned. Each student will take notes on the lessons presented by the other students.

After listening to presentations about three kinds of pollution (air, water, sound), students will try to redefine pollution. What is pollution? What is not pollution? A formal statement will be drawn for the teacher to review when completed.

Finally, the students will compile a list of the examples of air, water, and sound pollution where they live. If the teacher chooses, the students might also try to identify sources of pollution at the school where they are working and draft a memorandum to the student council suggesting solutions for the problem areas.

Author's note: In this example the teacher mixed two cooperative learning designs (share pair and jigsaw) to create a team of students who studied different forms of the same problem. The Internet is particularly good for this kind of activity since there are so many relevant sites for each student to examine. How do the Internet and the computer facilitate this type of learning?

PROBLEM-SOLVING DESIGNS

Since the ultimate goal of all education is to produce a useful citizen who can benefit by what has been learned in school, some curriculum designs focus squarely on the application of information to current events or real problems in society. In these designs, students are asked to analyze and synthesize large amounts of information and to skillfully apply their knowledge to the problems addressed.

 Journey — Natural Disasters

Grade Level: 7th to 12th

Activity Type: analyzing information and applying information to issues or problems

Search Topics/Keywords: Black Plague, Floods, Fires, Tornadoes

Outcomes:
   a. Students will be able to generalize across large bodies of data.
   b. Students will be able to distinguish similarities and differences in information.
   c. Students will locate useful information to address an issue or problem.

In this journey, students will visit Internet sites to familiarize themselves with the scale of human disasters regularly occuring on earth. Despite man's knowledge and capacity to find solutions to problems, disasters occur at regular intervals to mock man's knowledge and power.

In researching each of the four areas (plagues, floods, fires, and tornadoes), students will attempt to answer the following questions, which will form the basis of a required paper.

1. What constitutes a natural disaster?
2. What do most disasters have in common?
3. How are these four disasters alike and different?
4. What do we know about controlling these kinds of disasters that could be useful in responding to other natural disasters?

To gather information for this paper, the student will visit the following Internet sites:

Plagues
Plagues in Renaissance Europe
http://jefferson.village.virginia.edu/osheim/intro.html

The Black Death
http://www.discovery.com/stories/history/blackdeath/blackdeath.html

The CDC on Plagues
http://cdc.gov/ncidod/eid

Prevention of Plagues
http://www.cdc.gov/ncidod

Floods
FEMA Fact Sheet
http://www.fema.gov/library/flood.htm

The Oregon Floods 1997
http://www.teleport.com/~samc/flood1.html

Warning Technology
http://www.alertsystem.org

Prevention of Floods
http://www.pbs.org/wgbh/nova/flood

Fires
Great Fires in the U.S.
http://www.worldbook.com/fun/fire/html/great_fires.htm

Forest Fires
http://www.scd.ucar.edu/ug/FIRE/clarkfire.html

Causes of Fires
http://www.facts-1.com

Fire Prevention
http://www.worldbook.com/fun/fire/html/intro.html

Tornadoes
Facts about Twisters
http://www.usca.sc.edu/AEDC442/442984001/tkng.html

The National Weather Service
http://www.noaa.gov/er/wx/skywarn/patch.html

Tornado Tracker
http://www.gopbi.com/FEATURES/tornadotracker

Stormchase Center
http://www.Stormchase.com

The writing assignment is to assess the information presented, focusing on the four core questions, and to write an essay about the prevention of disasters.

Author's note: Problem solving is greatly enhanced by Internet resources and the ability of students (and teachers) to be in touch with one another via e-mail. How could e-mail be used in research or a problem-solving unit in your classroom or school?

CRITICAL AND CREATIVE THINKING DESIGNS

Curriculum designs that feature critical or creative thinking seek to develop skills in synthesis, analysis, and evaluation of data or to create new forms of knowledge which encourage the application of student imagination. Most curriculums of this type are futuristic or treat conventional knowledge in novel or unique ways.

 Journey — Methane Hydrates

Grade Level: 9th to 12th

Activity Type: creative thinking

Search Topics/Keywords: Air Pollution, Antarctica, Global Warming, Environment, Greenhouse Effect, Oceans, Underseas

Outcomes Students will employ creative thinking skills: self-directing questions, generalizing, perceptual scanning, understanding associations, model building.*

"New Energy Source Interests Congress" read the Associated Press story in newspapers across the United States in April, 2000. The story provided preliminary awareness of a controversial scientific topic, the discovery of a powerful energy source called methane hydrates. Essentially a crystaline solid consisting of a methane molecule surrounded by frozen water molecules, this controversial substance is found in abundance on the floors of our oceans and under the permafrost on the surface of the earth (*http://www.hydrates.org*).

For energy companies, methane hydrates are an exciting new source of fuel that might solve the problem of depleted fossil fuel reserves. Scientists believe that hydrates contain twice as much energy as the world's reserves of coal, oil, and natural gas combined. This powderlike substance is produced by combining methane gas

*Wiles Skill Clusters for Creative Thinking, 1980

and water under high pressure and low temperature. Test drilling has begun in Canada and off the coast of Japan, and major deposits have been mapped in Antarctica (*http://coolspace.gsfc.nasa.gov/nasamike/essays/vip/vip.htm*), the Gulf of Mexico, and off the coast of both Oregon and South Carolina.

The negative aspect of this story is a very justifiable fear that methane hydrates are dangerous to humans and may be the real culprit in global warming (*http://www.globalchange.org/center.htm*). Methane hydrates contain over 3,000 times the methane found in our atmosphere. What would result if these gases were suddenly released into the air? One government paper has even hypothesized that the warming of the earth during the late Permian Period might have released methane gases at high levels and caused extinction of flora and animals (*http://marine.usgs.gov/facts-sheets/gas-hydrates*).

Environmentalists are particularly worried about drilling now being initiated by energy companies and the hurried exploration for this new energy source. The composition of the earth near methane hydrate deposits is largely unstable due to the icy nature of the soil composite. Most exploratory drilling, to date, has caused landslides under the sea, thus releasing the hydrates into the air (*http://www.greenpeace.org./~climate/database/records/zgpz0687.html*). A secondary concern regarding such excavation is that it might release unknown bacteria trapped in the ice or under the seas for a long time.

Scientists from energy companies are working hard to determine how methane hydrates can be safely mined. Models (heat and mass transfer models) are being constructed to develop methods to maintain the cold conditions found 300 feet below the sea or under the permafrost at the poles. Meanwhile, however, drilling occurs unchecked in the Arctic (*http://www.gasandoil.com/goc/features/fex81086.htm*).

Student Responses:

1. What five questions would you like to ask about the exploration for and mining of methane hydrates?

    a _____
    b _____
    c _____
    d _____
    e _____

2. Of your five questions, select two which would probably lead you to a new understanding of this subject.

    a _____
    b _____

3. What is the connection between methane hydrates and other energy sources?

    _____

4. State the relationship between methane hydrates and the earth's atmosphere:

    _____

5. Are there any underlying assumptions in the information you have gathered that should be challenged?

_____

_____

6. As we think about designing a model to extract this resource from the earth, are there existing models or precedents that we should study (such as gas pipelines, blimps, and nuclear energy)?

_____

_____

7. In thinking about this problem, do any seemingly unrelated things come to mind (ice cubes, how diamonds are formed)?

_____

_____

8. Design and sketch a machine or model that would allow us to safely mine methane hydrates. (Use a seperate sheet of paper if necessary.)

9. Was there anything you didn't know that kept you from developing a model (such as theories of heat and mass transfer)?

_____

_____

10. State any nonconventional or wild ideas you might have about this situation that seem like "hunches" or feelings.

_____

_____

Author's note: Critical and creative thinking are not the same thing. Critical thinking has to do with putting things together and making connections, while creative thinking is largely intuitive and is about making unusual associations. Both kinds of thinking are extremely important in a rapidly changing, technological society. What occupational outlets are there for creative students in today's society?

SUMMARY

We hope that through these sample journeys, within different curriculum designs, you have discovered a design or designs which fit your teaching focus and the needs of your students. In the Resources A-E which follow, we provide you with useful Internet sites for classroom teachers, technology literacy standards for your students, staff development standards for 21st-century teachers, and steps for creating a web page at your school. Resource E provides 240 common school topics containing 1,200 educational sites for you and your students to explore and use in creating lessons.

If we, classroom teachers, are to become the true leaders in education, it is important that we employ the best resources available to improve student learning. We believe that many of these outstanding resources are available on the Internet. It is up to us to artfully weave these resources into learning webs which will capture the minds and hearts of our students.

READINGS

Fistering, Glennan T. (1996). *The use of educational technology: Elements of a National Strategy.* Santa Monica, Calif.: Rand Corporation.

Jonassen, D. (1996). *Handbook of research for educational communication and technology.* New York: Simon and Shuster.

Learning with technology profile tool. *http://www.ncrtec.org/capacity/profile/profwww.htm.*

Research Instruments website. *http://www.tcet.unt.edu/research/instrument.htm.*

SELECTED LEARNING ACTIVITIES

1. Using Resource E at the back of this book, locate five sites appropriate to a lesson about pollution.
2. Following the text as a guide, develop a mini-lesson on a familiar subject using websites to enhance your lesson.

RESOURCE A

Useful Internet Sites for Classroom Teachers

Blue 1 Web³n
http://www.kn.pacbell.com/wired/bluewebn

ERIC
http://askeric.org/virtuallessons/other.html

Help Web
http://www.imaginarylandscape.com/helpweb

Internet 101
http://www2.famvid.com/internet101.html

Kathy Schrock's Guide for Educators
http://schooldiscovert.com/schrockguide

LearningWebs, Inc.
http://www.learnweb.org

National Educational Technology Standards Group
http://cnets.iste.org/condition.htm

PBS Teachersource
http://www.pbs.org/teachersource.htm

Tappedin
http://www.tappedin.org

Teacher Pathfinder
http://teacherpathfinder.org

TeacherVision
http://teachervision.com.

Web Quest
http://www.edweb.sdsu.edu/webquest.html

Web Teacher
http://www.webteacher.org/macnet/indextc.htm

21st-Century Teachers Network
http://www.21ct.org

K–12 Technology Literacy Standards (NETS Standards for Schools)

PERFORMANCE INDICATORS FOR TECHNOLOGY LITERATE STUDENTS

Grades Pre-K–2

Prior to completion of grade 2, students will:

1. Use input devices (e.g., mouse, keyboard, remote control) and output devices (e.g., monitor, printer) to operate computers, VCRs, audiotapes, telephones, and other technologies.
2. Use a variety of media and technology resources for directed and independent learning activities.
3. Communicate about technology using developmentally appropriate and accurate terminology.
4. Use multimedia resources (interactive books, educational software, elementary multimedia encyclopedias) to support learning.
5. Work cooperatively and collaboratively with peers, family members, and others when using technology in the classroom.
6. Demonstrate positive social and ethical behaviors when using technology.
7. Practice responsible use of technology systems and software.
8. Create multimedia products with support from teachers, family members, or student partners.
9. Use technology resources (e.g., puzzles, logical thinking programs, writing tools, digital cameras, drawing tools) for problem solving, communication, and illustration of thoughts, ideas, and stories.
10. Gather information and communicate with others using telecommunications, with support from teachers, family members, or student partners.

Grades 3–5

Prior to completion of grade 5, students will:

1. Use keyboards and other common input and output devices (including adaptive devices) efficiently and effectively.
2. Discuss common uses of technology in daily life and advantages and disadvantages those uses provide.
3. Discuss responsible uses of technology and information and describe personal consequences of inappropriate use.
4. Use tools and peripherals to support personal productivity, to remediate skill deficits, and to facilitate learning throughout the curriculum.
5. Use technology tools (e.g., multimedia authoring, presentation, Web tools, digital cameras, scanners) for individual and collaborative writing, communication, and publishing activities to create knowledge products for audiences inside and outside the classroom.
6. Use telecommunications to access remote information to communicate with others, and to pursue personal interests.
7. Use telecommunications and on-line resources (e.g., e-mail, online discussions, web environments) to participate in collaborative problem-solving activities.
8. Use technology resources (e.g., calculators, probes, videos, educational software) for problem-solving, self-directed learning, and extended learning activities.
9. Determine when technology is useful and select the appropriate tools and technology resources to address tasks and problems.
10. Evaluate the accuracy, relevance, appropriateness, comprehensiveness, and bias of electronic information sources.

Grades 6–8

Prior to completion of grade 8, students will:

1. Apply strategies for identifying and solving routine hardware and software problems.
2. Demonstrate knowledge of current changes in information technologies and the effect those changes have on the workplace and on society.
3. Exhibit legal and ethical behaviors when using information and technology and discuss consequences of misuse.
4. Use content-specific tools, software, and simulations (e.g., environmental probes, graphing calculators, exploratory environments, Web tools) to support learning and research.
5. Apply multimedia tools and peripherals to support personal productivity, group collaboration, and learning throughout the curriculum.

6. Design, develop, publish, and present products (e.g., Web pages, videotapes) using technology resources that communicate curriculum concepts to audiences inside and outside the classroom.

7. Collaborate with peers, experts, and others using telecommunications and collaborative tools to investigate curriculum-related problems, issues, and information and to develop solutions or products for audiences inside and outside the classroom.

8. Select and use appropriate tools and technology resources to accomplish tasks and to solve problems.

9. Demonstrate an understanding of concepts underlying hardware, software, and connectivity and of practical applications to learning and problem solving.

10. Research and evaluate the accuracy, relevance, appropriateness, comprehensiveness, and bias of electronic information sources concerning real-world problems.

Grades 9–12

Prior to completion of grade 12, students will:

1. Identify capabilities and limitations of contemporary and emerging technology resources and assess the potential to these systems and services to address personal, lifelong learning, and workplace needs.

2. Make informed choices among technology systems, resources, and services.

3. Analyze advantages and disadvantages of widespread use and reliance on technology in the workplace and in society as a whole.

4. Demonstrate and advocate legal and ethical behaviors regarding the use of technology and information.

5. Use technology tools and resources for managing and communicating personal or professional information (e.g., finances, schedules, addresses, purchases, correspondence).

6. Evaluate technology-based options, including distance and distributed education, for lifelong learning.

7. Routinely and efficiently use on-line information resources for collaboration, research, publications, communications, and productivity.

8. Select and apply technology tools for research, information analysis, problem solving, and decision making in content learning.

9. Investigate and apply expert systems, intelligent agents, and simulations in real-world situations.

10. Collaborate with peers, experts, and others to contribute to a content-related knowledge base by using technology to compile, synthesize, produce, and disseminate information, models, and other creative works.

RESOURCE C

Preparation Standards for Twenty-First Century Teachers

The Teacher Will:

1. Use communicative technologies to redefine school learning.

   Provide each student with developmentally appropriate materials.
   Individualize learning for every student.
   Deliver learning experiences at the level of student readiness.
   Allow students to experience continuous progress in learning.
   Group and assign students by purpose, not progress.

2. Develop new and exciting curricula for students.

   Teach students the skills of access, assessment, and application.
   Stress an action-learning format.
   Be future oriented, focusing on problem solving.
   Allow for student choice and student expression in learning activities.

3. Feature new skills as a 21st-century technological teacher.

   Act as a guide and designer of learning experiences.
   Be the chief curriculum developer for classroom learning.
   Train and be trained by fellow teachers.
   Be a lifelong learner in the areas of technology and curriculum.

4. Develop evaluation measures that are relevant.

   See evaluation as a joint venture among teacher, student, and parent.
   Allow evaluation to assess the individual growth of each pupil.
   Diversify the source of evidence for assessing individual students.
   Integrate learning styles and preferences into evaluation criteria.

Reprinted with permission from The Association for Educational Communications and Technology.

RESOURCE D

Creating an Internet Web Page

Using Netscape Communicator (Composer and Navigator) on a Macintosh computer:

1. First, plan out your Curriculum Journey using the "Internet Lesson Planning Template" in your workshop folder. In completing the template, you will search the Web. Record the URLs of good Web sites to use in your Learning Web, and save any graphics from the Web to your floppy disk for use in your "LearningWeb"

2. Open Netscape Communicator.

3. Pull down the File menu to "new," then pull over to and release your mouse button on Blank Page. You should then see a blank white screen that says "Netscape Communicator" at the top.

4. Type your "Learning Web" Internet lesson in this screen just as you would if you were working on a regular word processor. There are two additional skills you will need to know to type in your lesson. You will need to follow the instructions below to *create links* and to *insert graphics*.

    A. Creating a link:
    - Type either the URL (web address) *or* the name of the site and highlight it by holding down your mouse button as you drag the cursor over the name or address.
    - Next, while the name or address is highlighted, click on the chainlink button/icon in the upper tool bar.
    - You will then see a screen where you type the actual URL for the link. In the "URL Location Box," type the complete address including "http://"; for example: *http://www.learnweb.org.*
    - Then click the OK button at the bottom of the screen.

    B. Inserting a graphic that you have previously saved to your floppy disk:
    - Place your cursor where you want the graphic to be placed.
    - From the menu bar above, pull down to "Insert Graphic" or "Add a graphic."
    - You will then see a screen where you direct the computer to your floppy disk and select the graphic ("gif" or "jpeg").

- Click on "OK" or "Insert" after selecting the proper graphic from your disk.
- The screen should disappear, and you should see your Web page with the new graphic added. Resize as needed.

5. Save your Web page to your floppy disk by pulling down the File menu. Name your document either "index.html" or "yourlastname.html."

6. Test your links and see how your Web page would look on the web. To do this, open Netscape Navigator by going to the File pulldown menu and clicking on Open and then "Page in Navigator." You will need to direct the computer to your .html file on your floppy disk.

7. Now you should be viewing your Web page in Navigator. The cursor should turn into a little hand when it is placed over one of your links. The links are probably a different color than the rest of your text.

8. To test your link, click once on a link to go to a site. If your links do take you to the sites, you correctly created the links. If your link doesn't work or you don't get a little hand, go back to Netscape Composer. Open the .html file and double-check your typing. Highlight the text link and see if you properly typed the URL. It is easy to make a mistake, especially with long addresses.

9. To move back and forth between Netscape Navigator and Netscape Composer, don't close or exit either program, but toggle back and forth between their screens. You can do this by going to the little icon in the upper right corner of your computer screen; it looks like a mini-monitor. Click on that icon and pull down. You will see all the programs that you have open and you can click on the one in which you wish to work.

10. After refining your page and testing the links, save your .html to your floppy disk again. Also, double-check to make sure all the graphics you used in the page are also saved to the floppy disk. Your page is now ready to be posted to the Web.

11. Options for posting your lessons:
    - Ask your county or school to post them to its Web site.
    - Post your lesson on one of the many Web sites that allow free posting of teacher lessons.
    - Post your lesson from your Internet service provider's site.

Topical Internet Sites for Lesson Planning

This section is a resource for teachers planning their own curriculum journeys on the Internet. More than 200 topics common to school curricula were selected and arranged alphabetically for quick reference. Each topic includes five Web addresses reviewed for their educational value.

Please note that Internet Web sites are often not permanent. Some of the following previewed sites may expire or become inactive. If you find such a site, simply go to another address or enter your keyword into a search engine such as Yahoo! (*www.yahoo.com*) and select a new site.

Aardvark

Habitat and characteristics
http://www.awf.org/wildlives/60

All you want to know about aardarks
http://www.zoomschool.com/subjects/mammals/aardvark

Earth pigs
http://lance.lphs.dupage.k12.il.us/stu_proj/mic_chem/final/aardvark/bio.htm

Aardvarks in the virtual zoo
http://library.thinkquest.org/11922/mammals/aardvark.htm

Aardvark's diet and habits
http://www.africam.com

Acid Rain

ABC's of acid rain
http://qlink.queensu.ca/~41rm4

Acid rain program
http://www.epa.gov/docs/acidrain/student/exp8.html

Laws and regulations
http://www.epa.gov/docs/acidrain/lawsregs/1rainindex.html

Frequently asked questions
http://www.ns.ec.gc.ca/aeb/ssd/acid/acidfaq.html

European school project
http://www.brixworth.demon.co.uk/acidrain2000

Acne

Baby acne
http://www.babycenter.com/refcap/72.html

American Academy of Dermatology article
http://www.aad.org

Food and genetic influences on acne
http://www.geocities.com/Hotsprings/Oasis/7001/causes.html

Prevention magazine on acne
http://www.prevention.com/healing/cond_ail/acne.html

Why people get zits
http://www.brainpop.com/health/endocrine/acne

Addition

Brain teaser that uses addition
http://www.eduplace.com/math/brain/index.html

What are Fibonacci numbers?
http://www.ee.surry.ac.uk/Personal/R.Knott/Fibonacci/fibnat.html

A speedy addition trick
http://www.scri.fsu.edu/~dennisl/CMS/activity/MM-calcw.html#CW4

Fun counting activities
http://math.rice.edu/~lanius/counting

Use addition to fly a plane
http://www.planemath.com/activities/pmactivities4.html

Africa

Everything about the countries
http://www.everythingafrica.com

Art, culture, and music
http://www.africana.com

Africa in a '74 beetle
http://www.stossel.ch/beetle_africa.htm

Pictures—top to bottom
http://www.jao.com/africa/index.html

East Africa safari by web
http://www.safariweb.com

Age of Exploration

U.S. Exploration and discovery maps
http://memory.loc.gov/ammen/gmdhtml/dsxphome.html

European voyages of exploration
http://www.acs.ucalgary.ca/HIST/tutor/eurvoya/intro.html

Using latitude to sail the world
http://www.ruf.rice.edu/~feegi

Interactive museum of New France
http://www.vmnf.civilization.ca/somn-en.htm

Exploring the explorers with students
http://www.hosps.nexus.edu.au/Projects/Explorers/List.htm

Aging

Findings and studies on aging
http://www3.oup.co.uk/ageing/contents

The positive side of getting old
http://www.seniorresource.com

Clinical depression of the elderly
http://fly.hiwaay.net/garson

Wrinkles
http://dir.lycos.com/Health/Beauty/Skin_Care

The employment of senior citizens
http://www.alaskaging.org

AIDS

The virus
http://falon.co.ukans.edu/~brown/virus.html

About the workings
http://www.pbs.org/wgbh/nova/aids

History of AIDS
http://www.aegis.com/archive

AIDS in Africa
http://unaids.org

AIDS in Asia
http://www.asiasource.org/news/at_mp_02.cfm?newaid=2861

Airplanes

Aeronautical engineering
http://wings.ucdavis.edu/Book/Flight/intermediate/aeronautics-01.html

Flight training
http://www.planemath.com/activities/pmenterprises/index.html

Virtual flight with the Wright brothers
http://hawaii.psychology.msstate.edu/invent

Design your own plane
http://www.phxskyharbor.com

Fly with the Air Force
http://www.af.mil/aflinkjr

Air Pollution

EPA Office of Air and Radiation
http://www.epa.gov/oar

EPA updates
http://www.epa.gov/airnow

Polluting industries
http://www.pirg.org/envion/energy/lethal98/index.htm

Indoor air quality
http://www.epa.gov/iaq

World without cars
http://radawana.cg.tuwien.ac.at/b~martinpi/nocar.html

Alcoholism

Danger signs of alcoholism
http://webmd.lycos.com/content/dmk/dmk_article_1456487

How serious is alcoholism?
http://webmd.lycos.com/content/dmk/dmk_article_5461917

Frequently asked questions
http://silk.nih.gov/silk/niaaa1/questions/q-a.htm#question13

Adolescent problems and alcohol use
http://alcoholism.about.com/health/alcoholism/library/weekly/aa000307a.htm

Blood alcohol content and DETOX
http://www.drsteve.org/drink5.html#na

Algebra

Algebra fun with a calender
http://math.rice.edu/~lanius/Lessons/calen.html

Quick math problem
http://www.algebra-online.com

Algebra jokes
http://www.stanford.edu/~meehan/xyz/girls4.html

Intro to basic algebra
http://www.mathleague.com/help/algebra/algebra.htm

Algebra vocabulary games
http://www.quia.com/custom/1312main.html

American Government

Declaration of Independence
http://www.law.indiana.edu/uslawdocs/declaration.html

Constitution of the United States
http://www.law.emory.edu/FEDERAL/usconst.html

Three branches of government
http://genxtvland.simplenet.com/SchoolHouseRock/song.hts?hi+threering

Signers of the Declaration
http://pages.prodigy.net/constitution/129.html

Learn about voting
http://www.headbone.com/derby/polls

American Literature

Webquests on American literature
http://www.edweb.sdsu.edu/webquest/9-12matrix.html

Thinkquest for the novel *Hatchet*
http://tqjunior.thinkquest.org/6224

More about American literature
http://www.csustan.edu/english/reuben/pal/TABLE.HTML

Specific works
http://www.cwrl.utexas.edu/~daniel/amlit/wallpaper/film

Mark Twain jokes
http://www.geocities.com/CollegePark/6174/twain_d.htm

Ancient Greece

Maps of Ancient Greece
http://www.princeton.edu/~markwoon/Myth/myth-maps.html

A visual tour of Ancient Greece
http://www.lausd.k12.ca.us/lausd/history/greece

The Minoan civilization
http://www.dilos.com/region/crete/ir_mus.html

Art, archaeology, and texts
http://www.perseus.tufts.edu

Ancient Athens
http://www.indiana.edu/~kglowack/athens

Ancient Rome

How long did it take to build Rome?
http://touregypt.net/wildegypt

Spend the day as a citizen of Ancient Rome
http://members.aol.com/Donnclass/Romelife.html#

Play Roman board games and ball games
http://www.personal.psu.edu/users/w/x/wxk116/index.html

Roman numerals and Roman math
http://www.cod.edu/people/faculty/lawrence/flash.htm

An illustrated history of the Roman Empire
http://www.roman-empire.net

Angels

Communicators of God?
http://www.angelaccess.com/frm/intro.main.html

Archangels
http://www.magicdesign.com/arch.htm

Good and evil angels?
http://www.execonn.com/stories/angel2.html

Satan and the fallen angel
http://zbh.com/sermons/falangel.htm

Quotes about angels
http://applecity.com/Angels/quotes.html

Antarctica

VIP tour
http://coolspace.gsfc.nasa.gov/vip.htm

Antarctica on foot
http://www.terraquest.com/anartica/index.html

The ozone hole
http://jwocky.gsfc.nasa.gov

Sailing Antarctica
http://www.victorycruises.com

Antarctica meteorites
http://www.a-v-t.com/antartica.htm

Anthropology

Ask a curator
http://lsbnature.org/curator3.htm

Museum of Anthropology
http://www.moa.ubc.ca/main.html

In the news
http://www.tamu.edu/anthropology/news.html

Anthropology e-museum
http://www.upenn.edu/museum

Searching for human origins
http://www.tnationalgeographic.com/outpost

Ants

Ant cam
http://www.discovery.com/stories/nature/ants/ant.html

The behavior of ants
http://iridia.ulb.ac.be/~mdorigo/ACO/RealAnts.html

Photo encyclopedia of ants
http://ant.edb.miyakyo-u.ac.jp/INTRODUCTION/Gakken79E/Page_02html

Scientific study of ants
http://www.myrmecology.org

Fire ants
http://uts.cc.utexas.edu/~gilbert/research/fireants/faq.html

Aquariums

Kelp cam
http://www.mbayaq.org/efc/efc_hp/hp_kelp_cam.asp

Play "critter match" at the Florida Aquarium
http://www.flaquarium.net

A virtual aquarium tour
http://www.neaq.org

Research and rescue efforts for sea life
http://www.mote.org

Bizarre and beautiful sea creatures
http://www.mbayaq.org

Aquatic Life

Aquatic and invasive plants
http://aquat1.ifas.ufl.edu/database.html

Institute of Ocean Sciences
http://www.ios.bc.ca

Information on oceans and climate
http://k12s.phast.umass.edu/~nasa/oceans.html

Marine and plant life
http://www.eos.sr.unh.edu

Clean oceans
http://www.cleanoceanaction.org

Archaeology

An archaeology adventure
http://library.advanced.org/tq-admin/forever.cgi

NASA's remote sensing research
http://www.nasa.gov

Petroglyphs
http://www.tamu.edu/anthropology/news.html

Virtual field trip to Mesa Verde
http://www.crowcanyon.org/EducationProducts

ElecFieldTrip_CRP/index.html

ABC's of archaeology
http://tqjunior.thinkquest.org/5751

Archery

The 2001 World Indoor Championship
http://www.archery2001.org

Archery in the '96 Olympics
http://www.usatoday.com/olympics/oar/oarm.htm

Archery around the globe
http://www.dcs.ed.ac.uk/home/ajcd/archery/links.html

Olympic bows and equipment
http://home.cfl.rr.com/pt/Archery.htm

Fundamentals of archery
http://www.users.nac.net/rfd/eoa

Architecture

Architectural periods to explore
http://dir.lycos.com/Arts/Architecture/Architectural_History/Periods_and_Styles

What is Googie architecture?
http://home.fea.net/~-ciensen/Googie.htm

View examples of period style
http://www.tulane.edu/lester/text/lester.html

View great buildings online
http://www.greatbuildings.com

Thinkquest on architecture through the ages
http://library.thinkquest.org.10098

Artists

Learn about many of the major 20th-century visual artists
http://www.1001.org/20th

Artist's lives and works
http://www.wetcanvas.com/Museum

Learn about art history
http://www.best.com/~natalew/main.html

Explore the major movements
http://dir.lycos.com/Arts/Art_History/Movements

Glossary of art movements
http://infoplease.lycos.com/ipa/A0106225.html

Art Museums

El Prado, Madrid, Spain
http://museoprado.mcu.es

The Guggenheim
http://www.guggenheim.org

The Hermitage, St.Petersburg, Russia
http://www.hermitage.ru/html_En/index.html

The Louvre, Paris, France
http://www.louvre.fr

The Metropolitan Museum of Art, New York, NY
http://www.metmuseum.org/home.asp

Asian Cuisine

Chinese customs and festivals
http://china.pages.com.cn/chinese_culture/customs/customs.html
Japanese manners and etiquette
http://homepages.go.com/~maizuru/FAQ-Manners.html
Meals in Japan
http://web.kyotoinet.or.jp/people/s1016kyt/ngk/meal.htm
Chinese eating customs
http://chineseculture.miningco.com/culture/chineseculture/msub_banquet.htm
Thai food
http://www.asia-discovery.com/thai_foods.htm

Asteroids

Pictures from space
http://www.bloomington.in.us/~jashoup/space/astro.htm
Information and facts
http://www.worldboo.com/fun/bth/meteorites/html/meteorites.html
NASA's planetary photojournal
http://www.as.wvu.edu/~planet/lnk_solr.htm
Impact hazards
http://impact.arc.nasa.gov/index.html
Asteroids and Indian legends
http://www.mae.mhn.de/comet/metlegends.html

Astronauts

The Apollo astronauts
http://mailbox.univie.ac.at/~prillih3/astronauts/mainpage.html
Women astronauts
http://www.friends-partners.org/~mwade/articles/womspace.htm
Ask an astronaut
http://www.starport.com/live/astro
To the moon
http://www.pbs.org/wgbh/nova/tothemoon
John Glenn
http://www.worldbook.com/fun/bth/glenn/html/glenn.htm

Atlantis

Fact or fiction?
http://www.activemind.com/Mysterious/Topics/Atlantis/index.html

Interesting facts
http://www.spiritweb.org/Spirit/atlantis-mu-lemuria.html

Complete works of Plato
http://classics.mit.edu

Atlantis Homepage
http://www.atlan.org

Where was Atlantis?
http://www.activemind.com/Mysterious/Topics/Atlantis/geography.html

Australia

Outback photos
http://come.to/australia

Maps of Australia
http://www.utexas.edu/Libs/PCL/Maps_collection/islands_oceans_poles/australia.ipg

Reef diving
http://www.laca.org/newark/wil/seminar/studentwork/aust

Virtual Melbourne
http://www.melbourne.org/melbcap,nsf/control+documents/home+page+frame

Posters
http://www.genesisfineart.com.au/index.html

Austria

Tirol and Alps
http://www.anto.com/summer.html

Hiking and backpacking
http://www.anto.com/hiking.html

Go Ski Austria
http://www.goski.com/austria.htm

Weather-88cams
http://www.tiscover.com/1root/Systems_homepage/f_homepage...2html

Salzburg
http://www.salzburg.info.at/rundgang/mo_geb_e.htm

Ballet

Ballet movements
http://www.angelfire.com/hi/Kimba2121/ballet.html

American Ballet Theater's Online Dictionary
http://www.abt.org/dictionary

The Nutcracker story
http://www.nutcrackerballet.com/libretto.html

The art of ballet
http://www.geocities.com/Vienna/Choir/6862

History of Pointe
http://www.geocities.com/vienna/strasse/5503/pointeshoes.html

Baseball

Ultimate baseball scoreboard
http://www.sportserver.com

History of the Little League
http://www.littleleague.org

Virtual Fastball Arcade
http://www.coloradorockies.com/pavillion/arcade/index.html

Major League Baseball
http://www.majorleaguebaseball.com

Sportsline Arcade
http://www3.sportsline.com/u/contests/arcade/index.html

Basketball

Ultimate basketball scoreboard
http://www.sportserver.com

Sportsline Arcade
http://www3.sportsline.com/u/contests/arcade/index.html

Read about your favorite NBA team
http://cbs.sportsline.com/nba/index.html

Player profiles
http://www.nba.com/history

ESPN NBA coverage
http://espn.go.com/nba/index.html

Bats

Stellaluna's friends
http://lsbnature.org/curator3.htm

Facts and fun
http://members.aol.com/bats4kids

Thematic unit
http://www.cccoe.k12.ca.us/bats/welcome

Interactive bat adventure
http://imagers.gscf.nasa.gov

Bat world
http://www.batworld.org/bats.html

Bigfoot

Fact or fiction?
http://www.netcomuk.co.uk/~rfthomas/bigfoot.html

California sightings
http://www.n2.net/prey/bigfoot

Sasquatch
http://www.cgocable.net/~rgavel/links/bigfoot.html

Where are the physical remains?
http://www.bfro.net

Bigfoot sightings in Ohio
http://www.suresite.com/oh/b/buckeyebigfo

Biochemistry

3-D images of structures
http://www.lvmsc.indiana.edu/educational.edindex.html

Virtual cells and movies
http://library.advanced.org/3564

A guide to biochemistry sites
http://www.biology.about.com/cs/biochemistry

Practice quizzes and labs
http://schmidel/bionet.cfm

Protein data and libraries
http://www.rcsb.org/pds

Birds

Caring for wild birds that visit
http://birdcare.com/birdon/encyclopedia

Read articles from the *Bird Watcher's Digest*
http://www.petersononline.com/birds/bwd/index.cfm

Track snow geese on the net
http://north.audubon.org

The Sibley and Monroe classification
http://www.stat.wharton.upenn.edu/~siler/birdframe.html

Bird brains
http://www.pbs.org/lifeofbirds

Birthday Parties

Great birthday party themes
http://family.go.com/Features/family_1998_05/famf/famf58birthday

How about some fun activities?
http://www.kidsdomain.com/holiday/birthday/party.html

Birthday party etiquette
http://family.go.com/Features/family_1997_11/ctfm/ctfm117etiquette

Great party ideas
http://www.birthdaypartyideas.com/html/party_ideas.html

Planning a theme party
http://www.boardmanweb.com/party/party_themes.htm

Black history

Museum of African American history
http://www.afroam.org/history

20th-century achievements
http://www2.blackside.com/Imman

Facts and questions
www.infoplease.com/spot/bhmi.html

African American exhibits
http://lcweb.loc.gov/exhibits/african/intro.html

History challenge quiz
http://www.brightmoments.com/blackhistory

Boating and Sailing

Interactive marine observations
http://www.nws.fsu.edu/buoy

A virtual ocean adventure
http://www.oceanchallenge.com/ca9697/classafl.htm

Sailing through science
http://goals.com/sailscin/sailscin.htm

Sailing information
http://Sailing.info-access.com

Boats and boat safety
http://www.boatsafe.com/kids

Bocce

Bocce rules and much more
http://www.ibocce.com

Strategies, tactics and virtual bocce
http://www.thedeli.com/THEDELI/fs_1.html

History of bocce
http://www.mindspring.com/~jlock/bocce.html

Bocce: on a roll in the U.S.
http://www.osia.org/pub/bocce.html

Great bocce links
http://home.netcom.com/~mifisher/bocce.html

Brain

The mystery of the brain
http://library.advanced.org/tq-admin/day.cgi

The brain connection to learning
http://www.brainconnection.com

Virtual brain tour
http://suhep.phy.syr.edu/courses/modules/MM/Biologybiology/html

The amazing brain
http://tqjunior.advanced.org/4371

Neuroscience for kids
http://faculty.washington.edu/chudler/neurok.html

Bridges

Build a bridge
http://www.pbs.org/wgbh/nova/bridge

Longest bridge over ice covered waters
http://www.confederationbridge.com

The Golden Gate Bridge
http:/www.goldengate.org

Covered bridges
http://romdog.com/bridge/brooklyn2.html

Brooklyn Bridge cam
http://www.mesc.usgs.gov/butterfly/Butterfly.html

British Literature

British literature resources
http://www.colonial.net/cchsweb/english/britlit.html

Authors and time period information
http://sbhs.sburl.k12.vt.us/britlit/accbritlit.html

British poetry 1780–1910 archives
http://etext.lib.virginia.edu/britpo.html

Medieval through 17th-century British literature
http://www.luminarium.org/lumina.htm

Butterflies

All about butterflies
http://www.EnchantedLearning.com/subjects/butterflies/allabout

Student's guide to butterflies
http://www.butterflyfarm.co.cr/farmer/bfly1.htm

Wings of freedom
http://library.thinkquest.org/27968

Butterflies of North America
http://www.npwrc.usgs.gov/resource/distr/lepid/bflyusa/bflyusa.htm

Children's butterfly site
http://www.mesc.usgs.gov/butterfly/Butterfly.html

Canada

Canadian Rockies video
http://GeoImages.Berkeley.EDU/GeoImages/QTVR/CanadianRockies/CanadianRockies.html

British Columbia time machine
http://www.bcarchives.gov.bc.ca/exhibits/timemachine/index.htm

History of Canada
http://www.cio-bic.gc.ca/facts/history_e.html

Canadian government
http://canada.gc.ca/howgoc/glance_e.html

Totem forests
http://collections.ic.gc.ca/totems

Careers

Occupational Outlook Handbook
http://stats.bls.gov/ocohome.htm

Self-assessment to analyze your interests
http://www.bgsu.edu/offices/sa/career

It pays to quit a job
http://www.usnews.com/usnews/issue/991101/nycu/quit.htm

***Working Woman* annual salary schedule**
http://www.workingwoman.com/salary

All kinds of salary surveys
http://jobstar.org/tools/salary

Cars

Traffic Safety Administration's ratings
http://www.go.com/Center/Automotive/Spec/Research_tools_and_resources_for_buying_a_car

***Kelly Blue Book* online**
http://kbb.go.com

Car articles
http://www.specialcar.com

Race Car Daily News
http://www.racecar.co.uk

Color a race car
http://www.coloring.com/working/begin.cdc?img=racecar

Castles

Architecture
http://www.castles.org/links/castle_links.htm

Legends
http://www.org/legends/index.htm

Medieval times
http://www.castlesontheweb.com/search/medieval studies

Castles in the United States
http://www.dclink.com/castles/INDEX.HTM

Castles on the Web
http://www.castlesontheweb.com

Cathedrals

Virtual tour of Durham Cathedral
http://www.dur.ac.uk/~dla0www/c_tour/tour.html

Notre Dame
http://www1.pitt.edu/~medart/menufrance/chartres/charmain.html

Washington National Cathedral
http://www.cathedral.org/cathedral

Westminster Abbey
http://www.westminster-abbey.org

Cathedrals of France
http://www.christusrex.org/www1/splendors/french.cathedrals.html

Cells

Bacteria cells
http://www.eurekascience.com/IDanDoThat/bacteria

Cell structures
http://www.kapili.com/biology4kids/cell/index.html

Cells Alive
http://www.cellsalive.com

Cell growth
http://www.icnet.uk/kids/cellsrus/cellsrus.html

Virtual cell
http://ampere.scale.uiuc.edu/~m-lexa/cell/cell.html

Chemistry

Chemistry for kids
http://www.chem4kids.com/index.html

The Atoms family
http://www.miamisci.org/af/sin

Chemistry basics
http://www.grin.net/~zgolden

Periodic Table
http://www.chemicool.com
Chemistry experiments *http://www.800hersey.com/history/milton_history.html*

Chess

Chess lessons
http://www.princeton.edu/~jedwards/cif/intro.html

Chess theory
http://www.infochess.com

United States Chess Federation
http://www.uschess.org

Free chess program
http://www.intersrv.com/~dcross/chenard.html

Play chess live on the Internet
http://www.chess.net/home.html

Children's Literature

Guide to children's literature
http://www.ucalgary.ca/~dkbrown

Authors on the Web
http://www.ucalgary.ca/~dkbrown/authors.html

The Internet Public Library
http://www.ipl.org/cgi-bin/youth/youth.out.pl?sub=rzn0000

Cyber-Seuss
http://www.afn.org/~afn15301/drseuss.html

Jan Brett stories and illustrations
http://www.janbrett.com

China

China today
http://www.chinatoday.com

Great Wall and Forbidden City
http://www.chinavista.com/discover.html

China's history
http://www.chaos.umd.edu/history/toc.html

Travel the Silk Road
http://www.interq.or.jp/tokyo/rrfujita.kenyuu/e_index.html

Find the provinces
http://lib.utexas.edu/Libs/PCL/Map_collection/middle_east_and_asia/China_Admin_91.jpg

Chocolate

The science of chocolate
http://www.exploratorium.edu/exploring/exploring_chocolate/index.html

Virtual chocolate
http://www.virtualchocolate.com

Wonka factory tour
http://www.wonka.com

Choco-Chemistry
http://whyfiles.news.wisc.edu/033love/choco.html

The town built on chocolate
http://www.hershey.com

Christmas

Send a card by e-mail
http://www.egreetings.com

Christmas songs
http://www.angelfire.com/bc2/donna/christmasmidi.html

Santa Claus online
http://www.santaclausonline.com

Webcam shots around the world
http://www.earthcam.com/holiday99

Poinsettias at Christmas
http://www.urbanext.uluc.edu/poinsettia

Circus

Barnum and Bailey
http://www.ringling.com

Circus fun
http://www.gardenbrothers.com

Clown gallery
http://members.aol.com/_ht_a/kechew/aclowngallery.html

Flying High Circus
http://mailer.fsu.edu/~mpeters/fsucircus.html

Circus parade
http://www.circusparade.com/navbar.gcp.lev1.htm

Civil War

1,000 Brady photos
http://people.delphi.com/yatsuo/go_main.htm

Lincoln's Inaugural Address 1861
http://ftp.mastate.edu/pub/docs/history/usa/19th_c/lincoln-inaugural.1

Battle summaries and descriptions
http://www2.cr.nps.gov/abpp/battles/bycampaign.htm

700 Generals
http://people.delphi.com/yatsuo/go_main.htm

Papers and reminiscences
http://jefferson.village.virginia.edu/ushadow2/personal/personal.war.html

Codes and Ciphers

Morse Code and phonetic alphabets
http://www.soton.ac.uk/~scp93ch/morse

National Cryptological Museum
http://www.nsa.gov/museum

Guide to cryptology
http://www.ftech.co.uk/~monarch/crypto/links/history.htm

Secret languages
http://www.exploratorium.edu/ronh/secret/secret.html

Cryptology lessons
http://www.achiever.com/freehmpg/cryptology/cryptofr.html

Colonial America

Colonial maps
http://scarlett.libs.uga.edu/darchive/hargrett/maps/colamer.html

Interactive picture of colonial life
http://www.pbs.org/ktca/liberty/perspectives/fact9.html

A historical almanac
http://www.history.org/almanack.htm

Continental Congress
http://rs6.loc.gov/ammem/bdsds/bdexhome.html

Virtual tour of the Freedom Trail
http://www.nps.gov/bost

Coloring Books

Interactive coloring book
http://www.geocities.com/EnchantedForest.7155

A to Z animal coloring sheets
http://www.allaboutnature.com/coloring

Wildflowers coloring book
http://www.nps.gov/plants/color

All kinds of coloring
http://www.thecrayonhouse.com

Color characters from the Book of Virtues
http://www.pbs.org/adventures

Columbus

Columbus' voyages
http://deil.lang.uiuc.edu/web.pages/holidays/Columbus.html

Journal excerpts
http://www.fordham.edu/halsall/source/columbus1.html

Culinary history
http://www.castellobanfi.com/features/story_3.html

Ships and navigation
http://www1.minn.net/~keithp

An ongoing voyage
http://metalab.unc.edu/expo/1492.exhibit/intro.html

Comedy

Good clean jokes
http://www.slonet.org/~tellswor

One-liners for kids
http://www.users.bigpond.com/lander/default.htm

Children's jokes
http://www.n-sf.net/cjokes.htm

Kids' jokes and activities
http://www.scatty.com

Puns
http://www.punoftheday.com

Comics and Cartoons

History of political cartoons
http://www.whistlestop.org/rk_hist.htm

Cartoon factory
http://www.cartoon-factory.com

Looney Toon picture gallery
http://www.nonstick.com/home.html

Comic strips
http://www.unitedmedia.com/comics

Comics on the web
http:/www.comics.com

Computer Programming

Survey of Visual Programming Languages
http://www.cs.berkeley.edu/~maratb/cs263/paper/node3.html#SECTION0003000

A Timeline of Programming Languages
http://www.byte.com

History of Programming Languages
http://www.scms.rgu.ac.uk/staff/db/Seminars/HoPL/sld011.htm

Programming Languages
http://www.cs.iastate.edu/~leavens/ComS541Fall97/hw-pages/history

From Machine Code to Java
http://web.dcs.hull.ac.uk/people/pjp/Teaching/082089697/Notes/Languages/node2.html

Constellations

Alphabetical list of constellations
http://www.astronomical.org/constellations/obs.html

Facts and charts
http://www.astro.wisc.edu/~dolan/constellations/constellations.html

Guide to observational targets
http://www.corvus.com/con-page/con-88.htm

Constellation quiz
http://www.mtwilson.edu/Education/ConQuiz

What to look for and when to look
http://www.dibonsmith.com/binoc_tb.htm

Contemporary British Literature

British Monarchy
http://vos.ucsb.edu/shuttle/eng-cont.html#british

Pictures of Princess Diana
http://www.go.com/Gallery/Arts_and_Humanities/History/By_country/Europe/United_Kingdom/Royalty

Official website of the monarchy in Britain
http://www.royal.gov.uk

Guide to the British monarchy
http://www.britannia.com/history/monarchs

Great monarchs of England and Scotland
http://www.genuki.org.uk/big/royalty

The house of Tudor
http://humlink.humanities.mcmaster.ca/~morton

Coral Reefs

Life in a coral reef
http://www.terryparker.duval.k12.fl.us/reef.htm

Tour of a reef zone
http://www.cyberlearn.com/zones.htm

Hawaii's coral reefs
http://thinkquest.org/J002237

Fisheye view cam
http://www.FisheyeView.com

Marine ecosystems
http://mbgnet.mobot.org/salt/index.htm

Cousteau

Legacy of Jacques Cousteau
http://www.aquanet.com

The person
http://www.incwell.com/Biographies/Cousteau.html

Cousteau Society
http://www.cousteausociety.org

Screensaver photos
http://www.webshots.com/photos/cousteau.html

Future cities under the sea
http://www.enteractive.com/jmcousteau/pages/tour1.html

Cowboys

Cowboy hall of fame
http://www.cowboyhalloffame.org

Autry museum of western heritage
http://www.autry-museum.org

Cowboy poetry and music
http://www.clantongang.com/oldwest/trade.htm

Pro rodeo homepage
http://www.prorodeohome.com

Tribute to champion bullriders
http://www.cowgirls.com/index.php3

Cultures

Cultural study—Nigeria
http://www.aghadiuno.afreeweb.com

Southeast Asian cultures
http://www.seasite.niu.edu

Cultures of the Andes
http://andes.org

SW Native American culture
http://www.desertusa.com/ind 1/du_peo_past.html

Southern culture USA
http://www.unc.edu/depts/csas/socult

Dams

Water power
http://www.fwee.org/TG/nwaterpwr.html

Types of water power
http://waterpower.hypermart.net

Hydro Electricity
http://www.eia.doe.gov/oiaf/ieo97/hydro.html

Grand Coulee Dam
http://users.owt.com/chubbard/gcdam/index.html

Dam issues
http://www.sandelman.ottawa.on.ca/dams

Dance

Many styles of dance
http://infoseek.go.com/WebDir/Arts_and_Humanities/Performing_arts/Dance

National Dance Council of America
http://www.ndca.org

Information on dance styles
http://www.sapphireswan.com/dance

Dance history
http://www.artslynx.org/dance/rsrch.htm

da Vinci, Leonardo

All about da Vinci
http://www.mos.org/sln/Leonardo

Explore Leonardo's workshop
http://www.mos.org/leonardo

Why is Mona Lisa smiling?
http://library.thinkquest.org/13681/data/davin2.shtml

Visit Vinci, Leonardo's hometown
http://www.leonet.it/comuni/vinci

Take a virtual tour of the Leonardo Museum
http://www.leonet.it/comuni/vincimus/invinmus.html

Deafness

Instructional strategies by grade level
http://monster.educ.kent.edu/deafed

Deafness-related legislative information
http://www.deafchildren.org/leg.htm

Communication options for the deaf
http://deafness.about.com/health/deafness/msubmenu3.htm

A world without sound
http://www.pbs.org/wnet/soundandfury

Growing up without hearing
http://www.gallaudet.edu/~nicd/565/565-1.html

Deserts

Egypt
http://www.alwaysadventure.net

Take an online safari of Egypt
http://touregypt.net/wildegypt

Construction of pyramids
http://www.gakkos.com/gallos/science/egypt/index.html

Famous cities
http://www.memst.edu/egypt/abusimbe.htm

Is the Dead Sea really dead?
http://www.mrdowling.com/607-deadsea.html

Virtually dig with archaeologists
http://www.website1.com/odyssey/home.html

Detectives

Thrilling detective Web site
http://www.thrillingdetective.com

Find somebody
http://www.anywho.com

Sherlock Holmes tricks
http://www.sherlockat.com

Famous detectives
http://www.hhpl.on.ca/library/hhpl/ra/famdet.htm

Research site
http://www.switchboard.com

Dinosaurs

Everything from art to tracks
http://www.isgs.uiuc.edu/dinos/dinos_home.html

Dictionary, video, and digs
http://www.dinodon.com/index.html

Electronic dinosaur book
http://www.zoomdinosaurs.com/subjects/dinosaurs/toc.shtml

An online egg hunt
http://www.nationalgeographic.com/features/96/dinoeggs

Build a dinosaur
http://www.discovery.com/exp/fossilzone/fossilzone.html

Division

Amazing Math Mania Theme Park
http://library.thinkquest.org/J002197

Play math baseball
http://funbrain.com/math/index.html

Division tricks and shortcuts
http://www.homeworkcentral.com/knowledge/vsl_files.htp?fileid=23053&flt=CAB

On-line division flash cards
http://www.aplusmath.com/Flashcards/division.html

Use division to complete a webquest
http://www.esc2.net/TIELevel2/projects/stocks

Dogs

Questions about dogs
http://www.k.9web.com/dogs-faqs

American kennel club
http://www.akc.org

Famous dogs
http://www.kizer.org/dogstuff

Dog screen savers
http://www.dogsaver.com/screensaver.cgi

Dogs for the deaf
http://www.workingdogs.com/doc 0005.htm

Drama

Drama teacher's lesson plans
http://www3.sk.sympatico.ca/erachi/index.html

Improv and games for the classroom
http://www.accessone.com/%7eup/playbook

Glossary of technical theater terms
http://www.ex.ac.uk/drama/tech/glossary.html

Method acting procedures
http://www.theatrgroup.com/Method

Dreams

The basics about dreaming
http://www.sleeps.com/basics.html

Dreams according to Freud
http://www.users.bigpond.net.au/dreams-genes

What are daydreams?
http://whiteshadow.com/DayDreaming.htm

Association for the Study of Dreams
http://asdreams.org/subidxedunightmares.htm

Nightmares and daytime fears
http://redrival.com/nightmare/about.html

Earthquakes

Stressed-out Earth
http://www.pbs.org/wnet/savageearth/earthquakes/index.html

Virtual earthquake
http://vcourseware.5calstatela/VirtualEarthQuake/VQuakeIntro.html

What's life like along the fault line?
http://www.exploratorium.com/faultline/index.html

Understanding earthquakes
http://www.crustal.ucsb.edu/ics/understanding

Living Almanac of disasters
http://www.disasterium.com

Ebonics

Oakland School Board's official recognition
http://www.tnellen.com/cybereng/nyt/12-20-02.htm

Teacher's guide to ebonics
http://educ.queensu.ca/~qbell/update/tint/postmodernism/ebon.html

Bilingual education funds ruled out
http://jobs.washingtonpost.com/wp-srv/politics/govt/admin/stories/riley122596.htm

Oakland School Board policy
http://www.personal.umich.edu/~jlawler/ebonics.lsa.html

Hidden meanings of black English
http://mbhs.bergtraum.k12.ny.us/cybereng/nyt/12-29-04.htm

Ecology

Wetlands
htttp://www.aquatic.uoguelph.ca/wetlands/chapter2/bogs.htm

The estuary
http://www.estuarylive.org

Coral reefs
http://www.uncwil.edu/nurc/acquarius

Rain forests
http://passporttoknowledge.com/rainforest/main.html

Ecology protectors
http://www.eco-pros.com

Einstein, Albert

Einstein revealed
http://www.pbs.org/wgbh/nova/einstein/mathematicians/Einstein.html

Einstein's major accomplishments
http://www.kingsu.ab.ca/~brian/astro/a2009a.htm

The works of Einstein
http://pup.princeton.edu/einstein

Man of the century
http://www.westegg.com/einstein

Einstein the brain
http://faculty/washington.edu/chudler/ein.html

Elections

C-SPAN guide to campaign definitions
http://www.c-span.org/classroom/lessonplans/campaign/campaign2000def.asp

Election history
http://lcweb2.loc.gov/ammem/ndlpedu/features/election/election.html

Iz and Auggie go to the polls
http://www.headbone.com/derby/polls

Who will be our next president?
http://www.pbs.org/newshour/extra/features/election.html

Project Vote Smart
http://www.vote-smart.org/reference/primer

Elephants

African versus Asian elephants
http://natzoo.si.edu/zooview/exhibits/elehouse/elephant/afrvsasn.htm

Picture gallery
http://www.tembe.co.za

Wisdom of nature
http://www.pbs.org/wnet/nature/wisdom/wild.html

Zoo trip
http://www.si.edu/organiza/museums/zoo/photos/phoset.htm

Elephant communication
http://www.elephant-talk.com

Ellis Island

Ellis Island Museum
http://www.ellisisland.org

History of Ellis Island
http://www.historychannel.com/ellisisland/index2.html

Stereoscopic images from Ellis Island
http://cmpl.ucr.edu/exhibitions/immigration_id.html

Celebrate distinguished immigrants
http://www.neco.org

Virtual tour of the island
http://capital.net/~alta/index.html

Endangered Species

Endangered animals and plants
http://eelink.net/ee-linkintroduction.html

Wildlife crime busters
http://www.nationalgeographic.com/world/9902/crime-busters/index.html

Animals removed from endangered species list
http://www.nesarc.org/delist.htm

Human impact on species
http://www.nwf.org/nwf/kids/cool/leopard1.html

Saving our wildlife
http://www.bagheera.com

Environment

Experimental Internet Global Environment Education Center
http://solstice.crest.org/index.shtml

View Earth from the shuttle
http://earthrise.sdsc.edu

Kids in action to save the environment
http://tqjunior.advanced.org/6076/index.html

Articles about the environment
http://headlines.yahoo.com/Full_Coverage/Yahooligans/environment

EPA's Explorer's Club
http://www.epa.gov/kids

Experiments

Edible experiments
http://www.madsci.org/experiments

Mad scientist experiments
http://library.thinkquest.org/J001796

Space experiments from NASA
http://www.wff.nasa.gov/~sspp/sem/html

Physical and life science experiments for all ages
http://www.spartechsoftware.com/reeko

Chemistry experiments you can do at home
http://library.thinkquest.org/2690/exper/exper.htm

Fairies

Garden Fairies
http://msnhomepages.talkcity.com/AquariusAve/annhawk

Fairy poetry
http://www.geocities.com/Heartland/Meadows/1322/poetry.htm

What is a fairy?
http://www.marskandiser.com/Fairies.html

Fairy poetry and art
http://208.195.115.3/angeleyes

1917 fairy photographs
http://www.lhup.edu/~dsimanek/doyle.htm

Farms

Kansas CyberSpace farm
http://www.cyberspaceag.com

George Washington's farm
http://www.mountvernon.org/pioneer

Ranching in Colorado
http://www.kidsfarm.com/where%20are%20we.htm

Farmers and the environment
http://www.topaz.kenyon.edu/projects/farmschool/addins/farmscho.htm

Agriculture links for kids
http://www.usda.gov/nass/nasskids/nasskids.htm

Fashion

A history of fashion time line
http://www.costumes.org/pages/costhistpage.htm

20th century fashion
http://www.costumegallery.com

Costumes and fashion through contemporary art
http://www.marquise.de

Latest Paris fashions
http://www.worldmedia.fr/fashion/indexva.html

Haute couture
http://www.metrofashion.com

Fencing

History and rules of fencing
http://www.pacificnet.net/~varon/fencing

History of fencing
http://www.britannica.com/bcom/eb/article/7/0,5716,34567+1,00.html

Fencing news
http://www.fencing.net

Fencing photos
http://www.tunkhannock.com/fencing/photos.html

Olympics Fencing
http://sports.yahoo.com/oly/fencing

Filmmaking

Independent filmmaking tour
http://www.tramline.com/tours/filmmaking

Super 8 filmmaking
http://www.super8filmmaking.com

The motion picture industry
http://library.thinkquest.org/10015

Online venues
http://www.filmmaking.net/cgi-bin/ifcont/static/contents.asp

Screen a web movie
http://www.webmovie.com

Fires

Great fires in the United States
http://www.acsu.edu/~dpuffer/greatfires.html

Fires of time
http://www.firesoftime.com

Fire prevention
http://www.worldbook.com/fun/fire/html/intro.html

Fire causation
http://www.facts-1.com

Forest fires
http://www.scd.ucar.edu/vg/FIRE/ClarkFire.html

Flags

Flags of all nations
http://www.theodora.com/flags.html

Songs and flags of our states
http://www.imagesoft.net/flags/flags/html

Other flags in America
http://plus.ua.pt/animfactory/factory/flags/indiannations/.html

International signal flags
http:/www.envmed.rochester.edu/wwwrlp/flags/flags.htm

Medieval flags
http://www.kwantlen.bc.ca/~donna/sca/flags

Floods

FEMA fact sheet
http://www.fema.gov/library/floodf.htm

Are you ready?
http://www.redcross.org/disaster/safety/floods.html

Prevention of floods
http://www.pbs.org/wgbh/nova/flood

Warning technology
http://www.alertsystem.org

The Oregon floods 1997
http://www.teleport.com/~samc/flood1.html

Flowers

Flower arranging
http://www.lhj.com/yourhome/flowers

Flower gardening
http://armchairgardener.com

Flower symbolism
http://mayflowers.net/symbolism.html

What does the passion flower symbolize?
http://www.mgardens.org/JS-TPF-MG.html

Victorian language of flowers
http://home.kendra.com/victorianrituals/Victor/flowers.htm

Folk and Fairy Tales

Listen to and read Aesop's Fables
http://www.pacificnet.net/~johnr/aesop

The Grimm Brothers' fairy tales
http://www.nationalgeographic.com/grimm

Classic and modern versions of tales
http://www.ongoing-tales.com/SERIALS/oldtime

Storytellers read aloud tales
http://www.childrenstory.com

Korean folk tales
http://www.lg.co.kr/kids/e_ani/n_guestroom.htm

Food Chains and Webs

Food Chains A to Z
http://edu.leeds.ac.uk/~edu/technology/epb97/forest/azfoodcw.htm

Food chains and webs
*http://www.highlands.w_cook.k12.il.us/Prairie/ecology/BASIC%20ECOLOGY/
    PREVIEW.HTML*

Ecology
http://www.kapili.com/biology4kids/eco/index.html

Rainforest food web
http://www.earthwatch.org/ed/pm/nickle.html

Build your own web
http://www.gould.edu.au/foodwebs/kids_web.htm#mystery

Football

NFL's site for kids with facts and games
http://www.playfootball.com

Flag and touch football rules
http://www.e-sports.com/usftl

ESPN's NFL scores and schedules
http://espn.com/nfl

High school football rankings
http://www.foxsports.com/highschool/football

Pro football hall of fame
http://www.profootballhof.com

Fourth of July

General information
http://www.netm.com/4th/index.htm

History of independence
http://www.fordham.edu/halsall/mod/modsbook.12.html

Virtual battlefields
http://www.geocities.com/pentagon/Bunker/8757/revirtual.html

American Revolutionary War
http://www.geocities.com/Heartland/Ranch/9198/history/revwar/revindex.htm

Celebration events
http://gurukul.American.edu/heintze/fourth.htm

Foxhunting

Foxhunting in America
http://www.mfhaa.com/abfo.htm

Foxhunting research study
http://www.mori.com/polls/1999/ms990715.htm

Rules and cruelty
http:dspace.dial.pipex.com/foxman

Foxhunting tales
http://rivendell.cc.uky.edu/Foxhunting

Vote for or against foxhunting
http://equest.remus.com/news/070100-02.htm

France

France photo gallery
http://www.raingod.com/angus/Gallery/Photos/Europe/France/index.html

Map of France
http://www.lib.utexas.edu/Libs/PCL/Map_collection/europe/France.GIF

French for kids
http://www.koronis.com/french/kids

Hear and read French
http://www.language-student.com

The country, people, and traditions
www.zipzapfrance.com

Frank, Anne

Her life and times
http://www.annefrank.com

Anne's house
http://www.annefrank.nl

Innocence in an age of evil
http://home8.inet.tele.dk/aaaa/Annefrank.htm

Anne's diaries
http://af.simplenet.com

Anne Frank Internet guide
http://www-th.phys.rug.nl/~ma/annefrank.html

Franklin, Benjamin

Interactive biography
http://sin.fi.edu/franklin/rotten.html

A kids' guide to Ben Franklin
http://bensguide.gpo.gov/benfranklin/index.html

Read Ben's autobiography
http://earlyamerica.com/lives/franklin/index.html

Anecdotes and quotations
http://library.advanced.org/tq-admin/day.cgi

A documentary
http://www.english.udel.edu/lemay/franklin

Freighter Travel

Frequent questions
http://www.freightertravel.com

Conditions aboard
http://www.traveltips.com

Schedules
http://www.freighterworld.com

Shipboard life
http://www.maxho.com/~frman/life.html

Aboard the *Aranui*
http://www.aranui.com

Frogs

The froggy dance
http://www.froggydance.com

Virtual frog dissection
http://george.lbl.gov/vfrog

Fact and fiction
http://www.exploratorium.edu/frogs

Frogs are fun!
http://www.csu.edu.au/faculty/commerce/account/frogs/frog.htm

Hear us sing
http://www.naturesound.com/frogs/frogs.html

Futures

World futures society
http://www.wfs.org

Futures problem-solving activities
http://www.fpsp.org

World environment in the future
http://www.future.org

Darker visions of the future
http://www.futurefate.com

Nostradamus Society of America
http://www.nostradamususa.com

Gardening

Gardening for kids
http://aggie-horticulture.tamu.edu/kindergarden/kinder.htm

Canoe plants
http://www.hawaii-nation.org/canoe/canoe.html

The telegarden
http://www.usc.edu/dept/garden

Virtual garden
http://www.vg.com

Worldwide gardening
http://www.gardenweb.com

Genealogy

Genealogy home page
http://www.genhomepage.com

Find your roots
http://www.rootsweb.com

Beginner's guide
http://biz.ipa.net/arkresearch/guide.html

Genealogy for kids
http://home.earthlink.net/~howardorjeff/instruct.htm

Ancestors
http://www.pbs.org/kbyu/ancestors

Geometry

Interactive geometry
http://freeabel.geom.umn.edu/java

Geometry flashcards
http://www.aplusmath.com/cgi-bin/flashcards/geoflash

History and uses of geometry
http://fp1.thinkquest.org/J002441F

Geometry activities and constructions
http://homepage.mac.com/efithian/geometry.html

Tessallations
http://library.advanced.org/tq-admin/day/cgi

Germany, Romantic Road of

Castles on the Rhein
http://wwwmediaspec.com/castles/index.html

Beautiful Rothenburg
http://www.rothenburg.de/stadt/e/stadt1.html

Festivals on Castle Road
http://www.heilbronn-neck.ar.de/burgenstr/seite2e.htm

The Black Forest
http://encarta.msn.com/find/concise.asp/ti=04656000

Neuschwanstein
http://www.neuschwanstein.com

Ghosts

Ancient Ghost Stories
http://www.eliki.com/ancient/mysteries/ghosts/content.htm

Ghosts and haunting apparition folklore
http://www.paralumun.com/ghosts.htm

Investigating apparitions
http://www.mindreader.com/opi/apparations

Theories about ghosts and spirits
http://www.unexplained-mysteries.freeserve.co.uk/ghosts.htm

Ghost Theories
http://www.ghostweb.com

Global Warming

Center for global warming
http://www.globalchange.org/center.htm

Climate changes
http://enn.com/special reports/climate

Global warming update
http://www.law.pace.edu/env/energy/globalwarming.html

Greenhouse network
http://www.greenhousenet.org

The future
http://www.enviroweb.org/edf

Golf

Golf etiquette
http://www.mrgolf.com

Golf hall of fame
http://www.wgv.com/WGV/library.nsf

Golf video archives
http://www.thegolfchannel.com/navigation/frameset/videoindex.htm

16,000 virtual golf visits
http://www.globalgolfguide.com

Play putt-putt
http://members.aol.com/edhobbs/applets/cgolf

Grammar

Grammar safari
http://deil.lang.uiuc.edu/web.pages/grammarsafari.html

Grammar gorrilla game online
http://funbrain.lycos.com/cgi-bin/shtml.cgi?A1=grammar/index.html

Grammar help search engine
http://www.grammarnow.com

Short daily grammar lessons
http://www.dailygrammar.com/archive.html

Most common grammar errors
http://www.webgrammar.com

Greek Mythology

Origins of Greek mythology
http://www.geocities.com/Athens/Acropolis/5065/greek1

Greek creation myths
http://www.pantheon.org/mythica/articles/c/creation_myths.html

The *Age of Fable* Online book
http://www.webcom.com/shownet/medea/bulfinch/bull1.html

Gods, goddesses, heroes and heroines
http://www.loggia.com/myth/content.html

A Look Back in Time
http://library.thinkquest.org/18650/data/frames/frames.html

Greenhouse Effect

What is it?
http://www.azsolarcenter.com/education/renewable011199.html

Global warming
http://www.enviroweb.org/edf

Global observations by students
http://www.ruf.rice.edu/~feegi

Taking action
http://www.worldwildlife.org/climate

Environmental Protection Agency
http://www.epa.gov/globalwarming/index.html

Guitar

Guitar tutorial
http://www.twinharbors.com/guitarnet

Guitar lessons
http://library.thinkquest.org/16098/ea/proframe2.htm

Music theory adventure
http://library.thinkquest.org/10764

Guitar chord diagrams
http://www.netexpress.net/~guitartab/guitarchords.html

Whole note interactive lessons
http://www.guitarnotes.com/wholenote/43-1.shtml

Heart

An exploration
http://medwebplus.com/obj/5493

The electric heart
http://www.pbs.org/wgbh/nova/eheart

All about the heart
http://kidshealth.org/kid/body/heart_SW.html

Watch a movie
http://www.brainpop.com/health/circulatory/heart/index.asp

Atlas of the heart
http://www.ama-assn.org/insight/gen_hlth/atlas/newatlas/heart.htm

Heraldry

What is heraldry?
http://www.heraldica.org

Glossary of terms
http://www.04.u-page.so-net.ne.jp/ta2/saitou/ie401

Coat of arms: British royal family
http://www.hereditarytitles.com

Symbolisms of heraldry
http://digiserve.com/heraldry/symbols.htm

Coat of arms for your last name
http://www.geocities.com/RainForest/Andes/8719/heraldry04.html

Herbs

Cooking with herbs
http://www.cookingvegetarian.com

Ginseng, Dragon's blood, St. John's Wort
http://www.open-sesame.com

Growing herbs in the garden
http://www.wvu.edu/~agexten/hortcult/herbs/ne208hrb.htm

The olive leaf
http://www.asktom-naturally.com/naturally/hsnltr.html

Herbs for a healthy life
http://www.nowfoods.com/herbs/sawpalmetto.asp

Historical Documents

Magna Carta
http://www.law.ou.edu/hist/magna.html

Law, history and diplomacy
http://www.yale.edu/lawweb/avalon/avalon.htm

Original manuscripts
http://www.rain.org/~karpeles

American memories—text and graphics
http://lcweb2.locgov/ammem/amhome.html

Holocaust and WWII
http://motic.wisenthal.com

Homework

Homework hotline grades 6–12
http://www.wvpubcast.org/homework

Ask a scientist
http://madsci.org

Cambridge library for kids
http://www.ci.cambridge.ma.us/~CPL/kids

Study skills
http://www.how-to-study.com

Ask Dr.Math
http://forum.swarthmore.edu/dr.math

Hubble Telescope

Pictures from Hubble
http://opisite.stsci.edu/pubinfo/pictures.html

Hubble Telescope
http://www.stsci.edu/2000125/sc/space_hubble_3.html

Hear the astronauts talking
http://www.discovery.com/area/specials/hubble/hubble/hubble/3.html

Make your own Hubble telescope
http://sol.stsci.edu/~mutchler/HSTmodel.html

Students select telescope targets
http://passporttoknowledge.com/hst/kids.html

Immigration

American Immigrant Wall of Honor
http://www.wallofhonor.com

Resources for today's immigrants
http://www.us-immigration.com

Irish, Jewish, Swedish, and Italian immigrants
http://library.thinkquest.org/26786

Asian immigrants in America
http://www.cetel.org

Immigration maps
http://memory.loc.gov/ammem/gmdhtml/sethome.html

India

History
http://www.itihaas.com

Languages
http://www.geocities.com/collegepark/language/5662

Maps
http://www.mapsofindia.com/link.html

Festivals
http://www.geocities.com/collegepark/lounge/5662

Taj Mahal
http://liveindia.com/tajmahal

Insects

Insect heaven
http://photo.net/cr/moon/insects.html

Characteristics
http://www.nysaes.cornell.edu/ent/biocontrol/info/primer.html

Nutritional value
http://www.eatbug.com

Collecting insects
http://hotrod.mt.ic.ac.uk/netsped/netspediton

Backyard adventure
http://www.butterflyfarm.co.cr

Inventions

Greatest inventions
http://tqjunior.advanced.org/5847/homepage.htm

Inventive research derby
http://ykd.headbone.com/derby/invent

Play invention games
http://www.nationalgeographic.com/features/96/inventions

United States Patent and Trademark Office
http://www.uspto.gov/go/kids

What is intellectual property?
http://www.yahoo.com/Government/Law/Intellectual_Property

Inventors

Inventors Hall of Fame
http://www.invent.org/book/book-text/indexbyname.html

Early U.S. inventors
Http://educate.si.edu/spotlight/inventors1.html

Index of Inventors
http://www.enchantedlearning.com/inventors

Innovative lives
http://www.si.edu/lemelson/centerpieces/ilives/index.html

Smithsonian's inventors and innovation
http://www.si.edu/resource/faq/nmah/invent.htm

Ireland

Irish history
http://wwwvms.utexas.edu/~jdana/irehist.html

The tragedies of Ireland
http://www.clevehill.wnyric.org/aphist/Irelandhistory.html

Saint Patrick
http://www.geocities.com/Heartland/2328/stpat.htm

Map of Ireland
http://www.lib.utexas.edu/Libs/PCL/Map_collection/europe/Ireland.jpg

The Irish Times
http://www.ireland.com

Irish Folklore

Leprechaun fun
http://www.usacitylink.com/lucky

Leprechauns and banshees
http://www.aurora.komvux.norrkoping.se/crumlin/remain/01/legends.htm

Where is the Blarney Stone?
http://www.jantacc.demon.co.uk/ire3.htm

Leprechauns, Fairies, and Mermaids
http://members.tripod.com/~pg4anna/Leps.htm

Northern Ireland history and folklore
http://www.due-north.net/due-north/

Italy

Orientation
http://travel.yahoo.com/t/Europe/Italy/essent.html

Culture
http://travel.yahoo.com/Destination/europe/countries/Italy/cult.html

Postcard from Florence
http://www.arca.net/florence.htm

Roma—Overview
http://www.lonelyplanet.com/destinations/europe/rome

Rome 2000
http://www.roma2000.it

Jazz

Ladies of jazz
http://www.ddg.com/LIS/InfoDesignF96/Ismael/jazz/jzindex.html

Jazz for kids
http://www.pbs.org/jazz/kids

Jazz in Chicago and New York
http://www.theatlantic.com

The Red Hot Jazz Archive
http://www.redhotjazz.com

History of jazz time line
http://www.allaboutjazz.com/timeline.htm

Jefferson, Thomas

Biography
http://www.whitehouse.gov/wh/glimpse/presidents/html/tj3.html

Quotations
http://etext.virginia.edu/jefferson/quotations

Jefferson memorial
http://www.nps.gov/thje/index2.htm

Monticello home
http://www.monticello.org

Declaration of Independence
http://www.leftjustified.com/leftjust/lib/sc/ht/decl/home.html

Journalism

Civic journalism
http://www.cpn.org/perspectives/civic_journalism

Robinson Research of Knowledge
http://www.robinsonresearch.com/LITERATE/JOURNAL/index.htm

Human rights journalism
*http://www.bestoftulsa.com/bestoftulsacgi/FrameIt.cgi?url=http://www.worldlymind.
     org/creelover.htm*

Journalism archives
http://www.mediahistory.com/journ.html

Yellow journalism
http://tnt.turner.com/movies/tntoriginals/roughriders/home.html

Kennedy, John F.

Photo essay
http://www.time.com/time/daily/special/kennedy

35th president
http://www.geocities.com/~newgeneration

Inauguration—swearing in
http://www.jfkcle.com/johnf.htm

Kennedy–Nixon debates
http://www.debateinfo.com/hall_of_fame/kennedy-nixon

Speeches
http://www.whitehouse.gov/WH/glimpse/presidents/Hml/jfk35.html

Kennedy Space Center

Welcome station information
http://www.ksc.nasa.gov

The Virtual Tour
http://www.inficad.com/~robsv/CCASVT/ccasvt.html

Discovery (sts-103)
http://www.nasa.gov/shuttle/resources/orbiters/discovery.html

Night launch of Discovery
http://www.ksc.nasa.gov/shuttle/missions/sts-103/images/medium/ksc-99pp-1476.ipg

Shop the KSC store
http://www.thespaceshop.com

Kites

Kite toys
http://www.intothewind.com

Kids and kites
http://www.sound.net/~buckchil/KKWeb/projects.html

Newspaper kites
http://www.clem.freeserve.co.uk

Make your own
http://www.searsportrait.com/family_fun/loads_of_fun/kite/kite_instructions.html

Wind conditions
http://www.aka.kite.org

Kruger Game Park

About the park
http://www.toursaa.com/krugerpark

Seven day tour
http://www.indula.co.za./body.htm

Eco-Africa
http://www.ecoafrica.com/krugerpark/sighting.htm

Elephants in Kruger
http://www.nature.wildlife.com/ele82.html

Kruger photo safari
http://www.africaphotosafaris.co.za

Kwanzaa

Information center
http://www.melanet.com/kwanzaa

Send a greeting card
http://greetings.yahoo.com/browse/holiday/kwanzaa

The seven principles (nguzo saba)
http://www1./sympatico.ca/Features/kwanzaa

Kwanzaa recipes
http://members.tripod.com/~nancy_J/kwanzaa/principles.html

Lesson plans for Kwanzaa
http://www.whyy.org/smc/allen/ZwanWeb

Labor Day

History
http://www.dol.gov

Events
http://www.raisinnet.com/labor.htm

History of American labor
http://www.unionweb.org/history.htm

Labor leaders
http://dir.yahoo.com/Business_and_Economy/Labor/History/people

Strikes
http://iww.org/strike/title.html

Languages

Phrases in 66 languages
http://www.travlang.com/languages

Language dictionary
http://www.logos.it

Speak French
http://www.ambafrance.org/ALF

Speak German
http://www.snowcrest.net/rcaguila/d1.htm

Speak Spanish
http://www.studyspanish.com

Leukemia

The Leukemia Society
http://www.leukemia.org/pages/19.html

1992 U.S. Racial/Ethnic Cancer Patterns
http://cancernet.nci.nih.gov/seer/Leukemia.html

Incidence and survival rates
http://www.pt-able.com

Risk factors from Mayo Clinic
http://www.mayoclinic.com

Leukemia cancer news
http://www.cancernews.com/leukemiainfo.htm

Understanding leukemia
http://www.intlihealth.com

Lewis and Clark

Maps and journals
http://www.lewisclark.net

Lewis and Clark's dog
http://www.pbs.org/lewisandclark/inside/seaman.html

Online base camp
http://www.nationalgeographic.com/lewisclark

Follow the virtual trail
http://www.ucds.org/LCWeb/lchome.htm

Travels through North Dakota
http://www.ndlewisandclark.com

Lighthouses

Links to American lighthouses
http://www.maine.com/lights/www_vl.htm

United States Lighthouse Society
http://www.main.com./lights/ushs.htm

Photographic journey
http://www.ipl.org./exhibits/light

Legends and lore
http://www.pbs.org/legendary/lighthouses

Guest accomodations
http://www.maine.com/lightother.htm

Lincoln, Abraham

Virtual Lincoln
http://showcase.netins.net/web/creative/lincoln.html

Works of Abraham Lincoln
http://www.se.selfknowledge.com/255.au.htm

Lincoln online
http://deil.lang.ucic.edu/web.pages/holidays/Lincoln.html

Lincoln for primary students
http://www.sicc.k12.in.us/~west/proj/lincoln

History of Lincoln
http://www.geocities.com/sunset strip/venue/5217/assasination.html

Literary Criticism

Online literary criticism database
http://www.ipl.org/ref/litcrit

Glossary of literary criticism terminology
http://www.sil.org/humanities/litcrit/gloss.htm

Guide to literary theory and criticism
http://www.press.jhu.edu/books/hopkins_guide_to_literary_theory

Literary theory
http://vos.ucsb.edu/shuttle/theory.html

Literary criticism links
http://start.at/literarycriticism

Literary Devices

Virtual Literary Cafe
http://library.thinkquest.org/17500/data/litdev/litdevA.html

Powerful imagery
http://library.thinkquest.org/10111/mainmenu.htm

Figurative language
http://www.netcore.ca/~gibsonjs/figlang.htm

Descriptive vs.figurative language
http://www.freedomsring.org

Rhetorical devices and literary terms
http://www.uky.edu/ArtsSciences/Classics/Harris/rhetform.html

Machines

Simple machines
http://sin.fi.edu/qa97/spotlight3/spotlight3.html

Making work simple
http://www.sd68.nanaimo.bc.ca/schools/nroy/grade4/gr4phys.html

Experiments with simple machines
http://www.galaxy.net:80/~k12/machines/index.shtml

Gadget anatomy
http://www.mos.org/sin/Leonardo/GadgetAnatomy.html

How things work
http://rabi.phys.virginia.edu/HTW

Madagascar

History
http://iias.leidenuniv.nl/iiasn/iiasn7/ellis.html

Maps
http://nationalgeographic.com/maps/atlas/africa/madagam.htm

Holidays
http://www.madagascar-guide.com/top/HP_FrlEng.html

Birds of Madagascar
http://www.inforamp.net/~ornst/madagascar.html

Eclipse of 2001
http://www.skypub.com/store/scienx/africa 2001.htm

Magic Tricks

Math magic
http://www.scri.fsu.edu/~dennis/CMS/activity/math_magic.html

The magic of Houdini
http://www.pbs.org/wgbh/amex/houdini

Tricks for beginners
http://www.conjuror.com/magictricks

Internet magic tricks
http://www.teleport.com/~jrolsen/index.shtml

Interactive magic
http://www.diamond-jim.com/magic

Maps and Atlases

3D Atlas
http://www.3datlas.com/main_co.html

Contour world maps
http://www.theodora.com/maps/new/world_maps_2.html

Map machine
http://www.nationalgeographic.com/maps/index.html

Find your street
http://www.mapquest.com

How far is it?
http://www.indo.com/distance

Marbles

Games we played
http://www.rice.edu/projects/topics/edition11/games-marbles.htm

Play ringer
http://www.blocksite.com/mcc/gm_ring.htm

Guide to marbles and collecting
http://www.blocksite.com/mcc

Marble connections
http://www.marblealan.com

Play Chinese Checkers online
http://home-cgi.ust.hk/~wwkin/ccheckers.html

Marco Polo

Travels in China
http://campus.northpark.edu/history/WebChron/China/MarcoPolo.html

Biography
http://www.carmensandiego.com/products/time/marcoc06/marcopolo.html

His effect on the world
http://www.geocities.com/TimesSquare/Maze/5099/sld001.html

Marco Polo and Korcula
http://www.korcula.net/mpolo/index.html

Travel the Silk Road
http://www.interq.or.jp/tokyo/rrfujita.kenyuu/e_index.html

Mars

Vital statistics
http://www.mpfwww.pjl.nasa.gov/med/science/index.html

The Mars Society
http://www.marssociety.org

Mars in the news
http://www.cmex.arc.nasa.gov.

Mars—science fiction
http://www.scifan.com/science/mars

Mysterious sounds from Mars
http://www.cnn.com/2000/tech/space/0127/mars.lander/index.html

Math

History of math
http://tqjunior/advanced.org/4116

First 28,915 odd primes
http://www.newdream.net/~sage/old/numbers

Myriad of math lessons
http://math.rice.edu/~lanius/Lessons

Math and critical thinking
http://www.eduplace.com/math/brain/index.html

Math in daily life
http://www.learner.org/exhibits/dailymath

Mazes

Cartoon mazes
http://ourworld-top.cs.com/mazoonist/index.htm

Interactive rat maze
http://www.sce.carleton.ca/netmanage/java/Maze.html

Amazing 2D and 3D mazes
http://www.gjnem.demon.co.uk/index.htm

Many mazes to get lost in
http://web.kyoto-inet.or.jp/people/eisaku/e_maze

Maze designer's page
http://www.mazemaker.com/index.htm

Measurement

Your weight on other worlds
http://www.exploratorium.edu/ronh/weight

Temperature and thermometers
http://www.unidata.ucar.edu/staff/blynds/tmp.html

Weather calculator
http://www.srh.noaa.gov/elp/wxcalc/wxcalc.html

Metric conversion tool
http://www.allmath.com/metric.asp

Metric system basics
http://tqjunior.thinkquest.org/3804

Multiplication

Learn how to multiply
http://www.tqjunior.advanced.org/3896/index2.htm

Multiply two digit number by eleven
http://www.learningkingdom.com/eleven

Online multiplication activities
http://schoolcentral.com/willoughby

On-line multiplication flash cards
http://www.edu4kids.com/math

Free multiplication worksheets
http://freeworksheets.com/sub_cat1.math.asp?cat=Mat

Musical Theater

American jazz dance in theater
http://www.jazzart.org/jdh/history/rootsthea.html

Cats **musical information**
http://www.reallyuseful.com/Cats/index.html

What were minstrel shows?
http://www.pitt.edu/~amerimus/minstrel.htm

Godspell—**the musical (rock opera)**
http://www.netpuppy.com/godspell/themusical.htm

Early musicals on stage
http://www.musical101.com/1860to79.htm

Nepal

Fast facts
http://www nepal.com/facts.html

Kathmandu
http://www.sirius.com/~echo/index 2.html

Trekking to Mt. Everest
http://www.wowadventures.com/html.nplmap.html

Trekking diary
http://www.talula.demon.co.uk/nepal

Himalaya photos
http://members.aol.com/mpokhrel/index.htm

New Zealand

Planning a visit
http://discovernz.co.nz

Maps
http://www.maps.co.nz

Infrequently asked questions
http://www.jgeorge.com/ifaqcontent.html

Parks
http://parks.yahoo.com//parks/international/new_zealand_s_parks

Holidays
http://www.nzway.co.nz

Noise Pollution

Effects of noise
http://www.nonoise.org/library/suter/suter.htm

Anti-noise information center
http://www.lhh.org/noise/index.htm

Music and noise
http://www.lhh.org/noise/facts/music.htm

Laws to control noise
http://www.4.law.cornell.edu/USCode/42/ch65.text.html

Glossary
http://www.soundcoat.com/Pages/glossary.html

Nutrition

Games and facts
http://www.dole5aday.com

Test your knowledge
http://www.kidsfood.com/left.html

An advanced quiz
http://tqjunior.advanced.org

Trivia trail with Tony Tiger
www.nutritioncamp.com

Food group creativity
www.agr.state.nc.us/cyber/kidsworld/coloringbook

Oceans

All about oceans
http://www.ocean98.org/ocean98.html

Ocean racing-pictures
http://195.13.20.54/homepage/frameset.asp?lang-EN

Research on the ocean floor
http://www.-odp.tamu.edu

Ocean currents study
http://www.ocean-currents.com

Ocean bookstore and gallery
http://www.oceangallery.com

Paris

Tourist offices
http://www.francetourism.com

Virtual museum tours
http://www.smartweb.fr/fr/orsay

Eiffel Tower
http://www.tour-eiffel.fr

The Louvre
http://www.louvre.fr

National Art Center
http://www.centrepompidou.fr

Parisian Architecture

History of the Louvre Museum
http://www.paris.org/Musees/Louvre/musehistory.html

Most beautiful avenue in the world
http://www.paris.org/Kiosque/mar00/507champ.html

Gothic architecture and art
http://www.historychannel.com/perl/print_book.pl?ID=20607

Notre-Dame de Paris
http://www.historychannel.com/perl/print_book.pl?ID=24746

Effiel Tower tour
http://www.paris-tourism.com/places

Parts of Speech

Parts of speech tutorial
http://www.uottawa.ca/academic/arts/writcent/hypergrammar/partsp.html

Virtual Literary Cafe
http://library.thinkquest.org/17500

Parts of speech through poetry
http://www.cesa8.k12.wi.us/it/webquests/Poetry/index.htm

Sultans and Sentences Game
http://edweb.sdsu.edu/courses/edtec670/Cardboard/Board/S/Sultans.html

Parts of speech and wacky web tales
http://www.eduplace.com/tales

Pestilence

Bubonic Plague
http://pestilence.uchicago.edu

Plague in Renaissance Europe
http://jefferson.village.virginia.edu/osheim/intro.html

C.D.C.—Plagues
http://pestilence.uchicago.edu

The Black Death
http://www.discovery.com/stories/history/blackdeath/blackdeath.html

Prevention
http://www.cdc.gov/ncidod/dubid/plagprevent.htm

Philosophy

Philosophers of the World
http://www.arts.ubc.ca/philos/irvine/eyntk1.htm#TR

What was transcendentalism?
http://ra.msstate.edu/~kerjsmit/self_rel.htm

Who was Confucius?
http://www.enteract.com/~geenius/kongfuzi

Dictionary of philosophical terms
http://people.delphi.com/gkemerling/dy/f.htm#fall

Beliefs of modern philosophers
http://www.philosophynews.com/whip/appethics/ARCHIVED/appethics200003.html

Planets

Virtual space tour
http://library.thinkquest.org/25401/data/tour/index.html

Planet simulations
http://Space.jpl.nasa.gov

Postcards from space
http://www.spaceday.com/postcard/postcard.htm

How much do you weigh in space?
http://www.exploratorium.edu/ronh/weight/index.html

Cool pictures and experiments
http://www.kidsnspace.org

Poetry

Poetry projects
http://www.eduplace.com/projects/poetrypost.html

Fluency through fables
http://www.comenius.com/fables

Idiom quizzes and exercises
http://members.home.net/englishzone/study/idioms.html

Newsletters of the world
http://www.eduplace.com/projects/newsletter.html

Spelling test
http://www.sentex.net/~mncadams/spelling.html

Pokemon

Does Pokemon cause seizures?
http://www.pokemon.HQ.com

Pokemon character biographies
http://cod.draganfire.net/pokemon/seriejpn.htm

English and Japanese Pokemon
http://www.pokemon.com

Dangers of role-playing games
http://www.crossroad.to

Pewter City Pokemon Center
http://www.pewtercity.com

Pony Express

1860 newspaper accounts
http://www.cnet.com/~xptom/tales.html

Basic facts
http://www.americanwest.com/trais/pages.htm

Visual images from Nevada
http://www.rougetrader.com~dave

National Park Service trails
http://www.metrogourmet.com/crossroads/w.bagley2.htm

Misconceptions
http://www.xphomestation.com

Pyramids

How were the pyramids built in Egypt?
http://www.pbs.org/wgbh/nova/pyramid/explorer/builders/html

Great Pyramids of Giza
http://www.verdenet.com/isis/pyramids.htm

The pyramid builders
http://www.geocities.com/Athens/Academy/7357/builders.htm

Methods of pyramid construction
http://www.touregypt.net/construction/construc.htm

Did aliens build the Great Pyramid?
http://www.europa.com/edge/pyramid.html

Quadratic Equations

Definitions
http://www.unican.es/sosmath/algebra/quadraticeq/bdef/bdef.html
http://quadraticeq/bdef/bdef.html

Solving Problems
http://members.tripod.com/~kselva/quad.html

Equations online
http://www.univie.ac.at/future.media/moe/galerie/gleich/gleich.html

Practice test
http://cnc.gnu.edu/modules/dau/algebra/quadratic_eqns/exercises.html

Real-world applications
http://forum.swarthmore.edu/dr.math/problems/elders3.19.96.html

Quilts

Make your own
http://www.skepsis.com/~tfarrell/textiles/quilting/quilt.html

American quilts
http://www.pbs.org/americaquilts

The role of quilting in history
http://www.americaslibrary.gov/cgi-bin/page.cgi/jp/quilt

Florida's history through quilts
http://dhr.dos.state.fl.us/museum/quilts

Smithsonian collection
http://americanhistory.si.edu/quilts/index.htm

Rain

Why does it rain?
http://www.whnt19.com/kidwx/precipitation.html

Meteorology Discovery Thinkquest
http://library.thinkquest.org/11641

What is convection?
*http://www.eecs.umich.edu/mathscience/funexperiment/agesubject/lessons/caps/
    convection.html*

USA Today rain information
http://www.usatoday.com/weather/windexr.htm

Doppler, satellite and forecast maps
http://www.rainorshine.com

Rainforests

Ecology sites
http://geocities.com/RainForest/Vines/1009/main.htm

Field trips and lesson plans
http://passporttoknowledge.com/rainforest/main.html

Statistics and photos
http://www.rainforests.net

Sounds of the rainforest
http://www.naturenet.com.br

Rainforest Workshop
http://kids.osd.wednet.edu/marshall/homepage/tropical.html

Roaches

Roach world
http://www.yucky.com/roaches

Facts on cockroaches
http://www.orkin.com/roaches/roachesindex.html

Caring for your cockroach
http://www.ex.ac.uk/bugclub/roach.html

Hissing Roaches
http://www.geocities.com/Area51/Nebula/6511

Pet arthropods
http://www.key-net/users/swb

Robots

How do they work?
http://www.thetech.org/exhibits_events/online/robots/teaser

Robot of the week
http://ranier.hq.nasa.gov/telerobotics_page/coolrobots.html

NASA's telerobotics program
http://ranier.oact.hq.nasa.gov/telerobotics_page/telerobotics.shtm

Control a robot online
http://www.remotebot.net

Design your own
http://www.tcm.org/html/galleries/robots/design/robot.html

Rock and Roll

Roots of rock and roll
http://www.pathfinder.com/Life/rocknroll/rocknroll.html

Rock-n-Roll time line
http://pages.prodigy.net/cousinsteve/rock/feat4.htm

Best rockers in the 1960's
http://www.sixtiesrock.com/index.html

The history of rock-n-roll
http://www.history-of-rock.com

Rock and Roll Hall of Fame and Museum
http://www.rockhall.com

Roller Coasters

Facts and IMAX movie
http://www.theatres.sre.sony.com/imax/thrillride/fun_facts.html

Amusement park physics
http://www.learner.org/exhibits/parkphysics

Interactive history of roller coasters
http://coasters.eb.com

Construction and safety
http://tqjunior.advanced.org/5384

Build your own
http://www.discovery.com/exp/rollercoasters/rollercoasters.html

Roosevelt, Theodore

The icon
http://www.npg.si.edu/erh/roosevelt

Man of action
http://www.geocities.com/heartland/pointe/3048/bio/TR/TR.html

Rough Rider
http://www.rjgeib.com/thoughts/roosevelt/roosevelt.html

Speeches
http://users.metro2000net/~stabbott/tr.htm

Pictures
http://rs6.loc.gov/ammen/trhtml/trhtml

Saint Patrick's Day

Customs
http://www.wilstar.com/holidays/patrick.htm

Blarney stone
http://www.irelandseye.com

Festivals
http//www.ireland.com/events/st.patricks

Greeting cards
http://www.marlo.com/holiday/p/patrick.htm

Irish toasts
http://www.islandireland.com/Pages/folk/sets/toasts.html

Satellites

How satellites work
http://octopus.gma.org/surfing/satellites/index.html

Track your favorite satellite
http://liftoff.msfc.nasa.gov/RealTime/JTrack

You be the engineer!
http://www.satellites.spacesim.org/english/engineer/dp000.html

Build your own satellite
http://www.thetech.org/exhibits_events/online/satellite

Solar Max 2000
http://www.exploratorium.edu/solarmax/whatis.html

School Violence

Columbine High School
http://www.denverpost.com/news/shot0312a.htm

Reducing firearms for safe schools
http://www.ncsu.edu/cpsv/firearms99.htm

Kip Kinkel's sentencing hearing
http://www.courttv.com/national/1999/1109/kinkel_ctv.html

Strategies to keep schools safe
http://www.rppi.org/ps234.html

News report details Columbine
http://ericanddylan.homepage.com/archives.html

Shakespeare

Shakespeare activity
http://topcat.bridgew.edu/~Kschrock/spring98/schottenfeld

Tour of Shakespeare's England
http://www.cesa8.k12.wi.us/it/webquests/tourguide/index.htm

Shakespeare's world
http://starbuck.com/shakesphere/Macbethhall

Complete works online
http://tech-two.mit.edu/Shakespeare/works.html

Sharks

All about sharks
http://www.ozemail.com au/~ bilsons/SHARKS.htm

Are sharks good? Quiz
http://www.nationalgeographic.com/features/97/sharks

Great white sharks
http://www.eng.utoledo.edu/~ icenere/gw/main.htm

Tiger sharks
http://www.boattalk.com/sharks/tiger.htm

Hammerheads
http://ds.dial.pipex.com/sharktrust

Short Story Writing

Teen writing
http://www.brick.net/~classact/npoetry.htm

Teaching students to write short stories
http://www.branson.k12/mo/us/langarts/assign/week4.htm

Personalized short story
http://www.connicomputers.com/java_sty.html

Writing exercises
http://diogenes.baylor.edu/Greg_Garrett/writing/exer.html

Various story starters
http://kidswriting.about.com/teens/kidswriting/msubject26.htm

Soccer

World Soccer News
http://www.wldcup.cup

FIFAs World Cup information
http://world cup.socceralliance.com

Effective defending techniques
http://www.soccercoaching.net/articles/article.html

Soccer through the ages
http://www.planet-soccer.com/soccerages.htm

The soccer rule book
http://www.mlsnet.com/about/rules.html

Solar System

Solar max and solar eclipses
http://www.exploratorium.edu/observatory/index.html

Tour of the planets
http://seds.lpl.arizona.edu/nineplanets/nineplanets/nineplanets.html

Virtual solar system
http://www.nationalgeographic.com/solarsystem/splash.html

Solar system scale models
http://www.vendian.org/mncharity/dir3/solarsystem

Eclipses
http://www.mreclipse.com

South Africa

Country profile
http://www.abcnews.go.com/reference/countries/SE.html

Complete Guide
http://lnk.yahoo.com/bin/query/P=south%20.africa

Travelers health information
http://www.cdc.gov/travel/safrica.htm

South Africa on-line
http://www encarta.msn.com/find/concise.asp/ti=016d8000

Kruger national park
http://www.sa.co.za/knp/centenary

Space—Interactive

Amazing Space
http://amazing-space.stsci.edu

Lunar Eclipse photo gallery
http://www.mreclipse.com/LEgallery/LEgallery.htm

Space images archive
http://www.seds.org/images

Astronomy picture of the day
http://antwrp.gsfc.nasa.gov/apod/astropix.html

Sky calendars and constellations
http://darkstar.swsc.k12.ar.us

Sputnik

Dawn of space age
http://www.hq.nasa.gov/office/pao/History/sputnik

The sounds of Sputnik in orbit
http://www.nytimes.com/partners/aol/special/sputnik

Overview of Sputnik program
http://www.nauts.com/vehicles/50s/sputnik.html

The astronaut connection
http://www.nauts.com/html.20000129165819541

Sputnik home page, Russia
http://sputnik.infospace.ru

Sri Lanka

Government information
http://www.odci.gov/cia/publications/factbook/geos/ce.html

Maps
http://www.lonelyplanet.com.au/dest/ind/graphics/map-sri.htm

Wildlife—biodiversity
http://www.wht.org

Travelogue 1997
http://wwwcocoanut.com/places/maldives.html

Photo album
http://www-math.bgsu.edu/~mabhaya/photo/photo_album.html

Stock Market

Investing for Kids
http://library.thinkquest.org/3096

Quick quotes
http://www.pcquote.com

New York Stock Exchange
http://www.nyse.com

Learn about the stock market
http://library.thinkquest.org/3088

Virtual stock exchange
http://www.virtualstockexchange.com

Submarines

Early submarines
http://www.geocities.com/pentagon/Quarters/7433

Photos and bios
http://www.chinfo.navy.mil/navpalib/images/imagesub.html

The silent service
http://members.tripod.com/rtree

Exploration vehicles
http://ussubs.com/lead.html

Caribbean submarines
http://www.caribsub.com

Subtraction

Lemonade Stand Game
http://www.littlejason.com/lemonade

Subtraction links and lessons
http://www.proteacher.com/100011.shtml

Teaching subtraction with Dr.Seuss
http://www.halcyon.com/marcs/litmath.html

Subtraction word problems
http://www.squiglysplayhouse.com/Games/Quizzes/School/Subtraction.html

Online subtraction flash cards
http://www.aplusmath.com/Flashcards/subtraction.html

Surfing

The basics of surfing
http://www.surflink.com/justsurf/features/learnsurf/intro/intro01.html

About the Duke
http://www.surfart.com/duke_kahanamoku

Santa Cruz Museum of Surfing
http://www.crusio.com/arts/scua/surf.html

Surf reports and cam shots
http://www.surfline.com

Pictures—surfing the world
http://www.surfingtheworld.com

Tea

The history of tea
http://www.sameoldgrind.com/teahist.htm

British tea times
http://www.chintzroom.com

The health aspects of tea
http://www.teahealth.co.uk

Does green tea reduce arthritis?
http://www.arthritis.com/health

Herbal teas—medical treatments
http://www.herbalcomfort.bc.ca

Teeth

Healthy teeth and gums
http://www.healthyteeth.org

Letters from the Tooth Fairy
http://www.colgate.com

About the tooth fairy
http://www.toothfairy.org

Brushing your teeth
http://www.saveyoursmile.com

Tooth brushes
http://www.lafrom.com/hygiene

Time

History of time measurement
http://www.timechange.com/3m

Evolution of the measurement of time
http://physics.nist.gov/time

Time travel
http://www.pbs.org/wgbh/nova/time

World dates and times
http://www.bsdi.com/date

Count down the seconds to any event
http://www.spiders.com/cgi-bin/countdown

Tornadoes

Facts about twisters
http://www.usca.sc.edu/AEDC442/442984001/tkng.html

The National Weather Service
http://www.nssl.noaa.gov/NWStornado

About meteorology
http://www.wxdude.com

Tornado tracker
http://www.gopbi.com/FEATURES/tornadotracker

Stormchase center
http://www.stormchase.com

Treasure Hunts

Mel Fisher's treasure site
http://www.melfisher.com

On-line treasure hunter
http://www.onlinether.com

Environmental concerns
http://www.seasky.org/sea6.html

Sea life down there
http://www.scrtec.org/track/tracks/f01600.html

Treasure hunts
http://members.tripod.com/~earth Ocean expl/links.html

Truman, Harry

Profile of Harry S. Truman
http://www.who2.com/harry truman.html

The president
http://www.whitehouse.gov/wh/glimpse/presidents/html/ht33.html

Truman Library
http://www.trumanlibrary.org

Speeches
http://history.hanover.edu/20th/truman.htm

Twentieth Century

American history timeline
http://historytimeline.com

A century of photographs
http://www.pbs.org/ktca/americanphotography

American cultural history
http://www.nhmccd.edu/contracts/lrc/kc/decades.html

Presidents of the 20th century
http://www.pbs.org/wgbh/amex/presidents/indexjs.html

Timeline of scientific achievements
http://www.pbs.org/transistor/timeline/index.html

UFOs

Project Bluebook cover-ups
http://www.tje.net/para/documents/bluebook_unknowns/index.html

Fort Monmouth sightings
http://members.tripod.com/~AlienConspiracy/sightings/monmouth.htm

Hall of UFO Mysteries
http://unmuseum.mus.pa.us/ufo.htm

Sightings
http://www.sightings.com/ufo4/nasaknows.htm

UFOs in the Old Testament
http://www.geocities.com/Athens/Atlantis/5469/oldtestament.html

Underground Railroad

All aboard
http://www.cr.nps.gov/nr/underground

Slave narratives
http://vi.uh.edu/pages/mintz/primary.htm

Songs of freedom
http://www.ushistory.com/railr.htm

Follow the drinking gourd
http://quest.arc.nasa.gov/itc/special/mlk/drink.html

A journey by night
http://www.nationalgeographic.com/features/99/railroad

Undersea Environment

What's down there?
http://www.scrtec.org/track/tracks/f01600.html

Environmental concerns
http://www.seasky.org/sea6.html

The environmentalist position
http://www.bsac.com/world/nature/naturenews.htm

Battleground in the Artic
http://dailynews.yahoo.com/h/ap/20000324/bs/artic_conflict_1.html

Coral reefs condition
http://state-of-coast.nosa.gov/bulletins/html/crf_08/expert.html

Valentines

About Valentine's Day
http://www.newadvent.org/cathen/15254a.html

Free Cards
http://www.bluemountain.com

Poetry and words of love
www.geocities.com/-abelle/valentine

Romantic dinners and treats
www.kitchenlink.com/cupid.html

Say I love you—100 languages
http://www.dina.kvl.dk/~ fischer/alt.romance/language.html

Vikings

Runes, sagas, and history
http://www.pastforward.co.uk/vikings

Viking explorations
http://www.carmensandiego.com/products/time/vikings03/ebmain_c03.html

Viking explorers
http://www.mariner.org/age/vikingexp.html

Vikings
http://www.vikinger.dk

Viking ships
http://www.sciam.com/1998/0298issue/0298hale.html

Vocabulary

Funster multiplayer word game
http://www.funster.com

Cool word of the day
http://features.learningkingdom.com/word

Word Game of the day
http://www.m-w.com/game

Online dictionaries
http://www.surfnetkids.com/dictionary.htm

Winning with words
http://library.thinkquest.org/10623

Volcanoes

Can they be useful?
http://vulcan.wr.usgs.gov/LivingWith/PlusSide/geothermal.htm

Volcanoes in space and underwater
http://users.netlink.com.au/~jhallett/volcanoes.htm

U.S. volcanoes
http://pubs.usgs.gov/gip/volcus/index.html

Cinder cone volcanoes
http://volcanoes.usgs.gov/Products/Pglossary/CinderCone.html

Ring of Fire
http://vulcan.wr.usgs.gov/Glossary/PlateTectonics/description_plate_tectonics.html

Washington, George

The first president
http:/www.whitehouse.gov/wh/glimpse/presidents/html/gw1.html

George Washington links
http://www.geocities.com/Athens/Acropolis/465/gwlinks.html

Mount Vernon
http://www.mountvernon.org

George Washington's journal
http://209.54.40.178/earlyamerica/milestones/journals/index.html

Life of George Washington
http://www.earlyamerica.com/lives/gwlife

Waste Management

Superfund for kids
http://www.epa.gov/superfund/kids

Hazardous substances
http://www.atsdr.cdc.gov/toxfaq.html

Household hazards
http://outreach.missouri.edu/owm/hhw.htm

Toxic substances
http://www.atsdr.cdc.gov/atsdhome.html

Garbage
http://www.learner.org/exhibits/garbage

Water Pollution

Water pollution
http://www.ukrivers.net/pollution.html

Guide to contaminants
http://www.time.com/time/reports/environment/heroes/contaminants

Don't flush this
http://wsa.co.uk

MTBE-frequently asked questions
http://www.epa.gov/swerust 1/mtbe/index.htm

MBTE in drinking water
http://epa.gov/safewater/mtbe.html

Weather

Wild weather
http://www.whnt19.com/kidwx/index.html

Hurricanes
http://www.miamisci.org/hurricane/hurricane0.html

National Weather Service
http://www.nws.noaa.gov

All about weather
http://weather.apoke.com/storms.html

Weather activities
http://www.learner.org/exhibits/weather

Wedding Customs

Superstitions
http://weddings.co.uic/info/tradsupe.htm

Japanese weddings
http://www.Japan-guide.com/e/e2061.html

Jewish weddings
http://weddingcircle.com/ethnic/jewish

African weddings
http://melanet.com/awg

Scottish weddings
http://weddingcircle.com/ethnic/scot

Westward Expansion—United States

Lewis and Clark
http://www.pbs.org/lewisandclark

Pony Express
http://www.xphomestation.com

The way west
http://www.pbs.org/weta/thewest

The end of the Oregon Trail
http://www.teleport.com/~eotic

California gold rush
http://www.acusd.edu/~jross/goldrush.html

Whales

Beluga whale video
http://www.wcs.org/zoos/aquarium/aqanimals.beluga.htm

Thematic Unit on whales
http://curry.edschool.Virginia.EDU/go/Whales

The songs of whales
http://newport.pmel.noaa.gov/whales/whale-calls.html

The Virtual Whale Project
http://www.cs.sfu.ca/research/Whales

All about whales
http://www.EnchantedLearning.com/subjects/whales

White House

Planning a visit
http://www.whitehouse.gov/wh

Daily press releases/correspondence
http://www.pub.whitehouse.gov/uri-res

Presidential tapes—John F. Kennedy
http://www.c-span.org

Chelsea Clinton's pet peeves
http://www.ai.mit.edu/extra/topten/old95/list36.html

White House millenium projects
http://www.whitehouse.gov/initiatives/millenium

World Literature

Anne Frank timeline adventure
http://www.fsu.edu/~Candl/ENGLISH/fsuwebquest3/annef.htm

Homer's *Illiad* and *Odyssey*
http://library.thinkquest.org/19300

Shakespeare and his plays
http://www.thinkquest.org/php/lib/cat_show.php3?cat_id=82

Learn about Asian writers
http://library.thinkquest.org/23476

World literature literary criticism
http://www.ipl.org/ref/litcrit

World Religion

64 world faiths and ethical systems
http://www.religioustolerance.org/welcome.htm#new

Many world faith descriptions
http://www.nmia.com/~sundance/spirit.html

World religion index
http://wri.leaderu.com

Teaching and learning about religion
http://www.wabashcenter.wabash.edu/Internet/worldrel.htm

Comparative analysis
http://www.comparativereligion.com/index.html

Worms

The world of worms
http://www.yucky.com/worm

Adventures of Herman the Worm
http://www.urbanext.uiuc.edu/worms

Segmented Worms
http://www.ucmp.berkeley.edu/annelida/annelida.html

Worms of the deep sea
http://www.ocean.udel.edu/deepsea/level-1/creature/creature.html

Recipe for worm cake!
http://cakerecipe.com/az/WormCake.asp

Zebras

About zebra stripes
http://www.alumni.caltech.edu/~kanter/zebras/pictures.html

Grevy's zebras
http://zoo.interaccess.com/tour/factsheets/mammals/grevys_zebra.htm

When do zebras sleep?
http://www.2.wildfire.com/~ag/zebras.html

Zebras in love
http://www.hedweb.com/animag/zebrakis.htm

Breeding special zebras
http://www.smhc.com